Social Innovation in Africa

Rapid population growth across Africa poses major challenges for the provision of food, housing, education, healthcare, energy, transportation, water, and sanitation. Social innovators and entrepreneurs in Africa are leading the charge to address Africa's mounting challenges by developing and deploying new solutions to tackle serious social problems, where the value created accrues primarily to society. Despite their early successes, most interventions reach hundreds and even thousands, but struggle to achieve impact at the necessary scale by reaching millions of people across the continent.

Encouraged by the emergence and early impact of social innovators on the African Continent, but frustrated by the slow pace of large scale change, this book is focused on filling the knowledge gap among aspiring and emerging social innovators. It lays out the required building blocks including creating clear mission, vision, and values statements. It presents business models that are demand-driven, simple, and low-cost, with compelling measurement and evaluation tools that leverage technology. It also explores the steps for attracting and retaining talent and financing and forming strategic partnerships with the private, public, and non-profit sectors to foster scaling.

Using practical case studies, the book provides inspiration for those who seek to become innovators or to be employed by them, empowering them to scale their initiatives to meet the needs of Africa's growing population. Finally, it outlines the crucial steps for key stakeholders to take in order to support the emergence of more social innovators on the African continent, create an enabling environment for the scaling of high-impact initiatives, and advance collective efforts to build stronger communities for current and future generations.

Ndidi Okonkwo Nwuneli is a serial social entrepreneur based in Nigeria. She is the founder of LEAP Africa, co-founder of AACE Foods, director at Sahel Capital and in 2015, she was a Senior Fellow at the Mossavar-Rahmani Center for Business & Government, Harvard Kennedy School, USA. She has a MBA from Harvard Business School and Bachelor of Science in Economics Degree from the Wharton School of the University of Pennsylvania. She started her career as a management consultant with McKinsey & Company, working in their Chicago, New York and Johannesburg Offices. Ndidi was recognized as a Young Global

Leader by the World Economic Forum and received a National Honor – Member of the Federal Republic from the Nigerian Government. She was listed as one of the 20 Youngest Power African Women by Forbes. She serves on numerous international and local boards including Nestlé Nigeria Plc., Nigerian Breweries Plc., Cornerstone Insurance Plc. and USAID's Advisory Committee on Voluntary Foreign Aid.

"This is a brilliant book on scaling up social innovation and entrepreneurship, with relevance for Africa and far beyond. It presents an excellent analytical framework, wide ranging evidence of specific social enterprises, and practical guidance for social entrepreneurs and their partners. The author uniquely combines thorough literature research and on-the-ground interviews with her own rich experience as a serial social entrepreneur in Nigeria."

– Johannes F. Linn, Brookings Institution,
USA and Emerging Markets Forum

"Ndidi Okonkwo Nwuneli's has written a highly readable and useful primer for those seeking to scale high-impact entrepreneurial ventures in a highly diverse African context. As reflected in its title, this is a practical guide that begins by delineating the challenges facing entrepreneurial companies and non-profits that are unique to this continent, one where each country differs in its historical, political, social and economic background. While acknowledging these differences, Nwuneli is able to dive deep into the critical steps any social venture needs to take – whether in Africa or elsewhere – to safeguard the venture's legitimacy, reputation, financial sustainability and impact on the lives of its clients. The author highlights these steps with specific examples of high-impact ventures that continue to learn as they scale. *Social Innovation in Africa: A practical guide for scaling impact* is an important contribution to a growing trend among entrepreneurs that seek to combine business and social goals to transform systems and practices with negative consequences for individuals, communities and countries."

– Pamela Hartigan, Skoll Centre for Social Entrepreneurship,
Saïd Business School, University of Oxford, UK

"While Ndidi hasn't succeeded in getting herself out of a job, this first effort to reflect on scaling up social innovation in the Continent provides the nuts and bolts of doing so. Funders, governments, social innovators and civil society have much to learn from this book.

– Kole Shettima, MacArthur Foundation, Nigeria

"Rather than dwell on the barriers only, or tell a story of a few hard-to-replicate successes, this book concentrates on what could practically and immediately support scaling our local social innovations – by understanding the ecosystem and resources available on and to the continent. If you're advancing social innovation in your communities, your organization, your sectors or your country, this book presents a comprehensive review of the frameworks of thinking, the key pieces of the puzzle, and, through a rich journey of interviews, unpacks insights into some fascinating cases on the continent. Ndidi's path continues to be one of action, and through that, an inspiration to others in Africa – and now her gift to us all is a guide to make our own paths wider, to make them go further, intersecting with others as we join her call."

– François Bonnici, Bertha Centre for Social Innovation and
Entrepreneurship, University of Cape Town, South Africa

"Social innovation is a term that conjures up mystery. Drawing from her vast experiences as a serial entrepreneur, Ndidi Nwuneli has written an excellent handbook both for the perplexed and the curious. *Social Innovation in Africa* is as practical as it is inspirational."

– Calestous Juma, Harvard Kennedy School, USA and author of
Innovation and Its Enemies: Why People Resist New Technologies

Routledge Studies in African Development

Social Innovation in Africa
A practical guide for scaling impact

Ndidi Okonkwo Nwuneli

Routledge
Taylor & Francis Group

LONDON AND NEW YORK

earthscan
from Routledge

First published 2016
by Routledge
2 Park Square, Milton Park, Abingdon, Oxon OX14 4RN

and by Routledge
711 Third Avenue, New York, NY 10017

Routledge is an imprint of the Taylor & Francis Group, an informa business

British Library Cataloguing-in-Publication Data
A catalogue record for this book is available from the British Library

Library of Congress Cataloging in Publication Data
Names: Nwuneli, Ndidi Okonkwo, author.Title: Social innovation in
Africa : a practical guide for scaling impact / Ndidi Okonkwo Nwuneli.
Description: New York : Routledge, 2016. | Series: Routledge studies in
african development | Includes bibliographical references and index.
Identifiers: LCCN 2015050306| ISBN 9781138182806 (hbk) | ISBN
9781138182844 (pbk) | ISBN 9781315646190 (ebk)Subjects: LCSH:
Social entrepreneurship--Africa. | Social change--Africa. | Social
responsibility of business--Africa. | Strategic planning--Africa.Classification:
LCC HD60.5.A35 N98 2016 | DDC 338/.04096--dc23LC record available
at https://lccn.loc.gov/2015050306

ISBN: 978-1-138-18280-6 (hbk)
ISBN: 978-1-138-18284-4 (pbk)
ISBN: 978-1-315-64619-0 (ebk)

Typeset in Goudy
by Fish Books Ltd.

For Amara and Udenna – and the countless other African children for whom we strive.

Contents

List of illustrations

Figures

Tables

Boxes (Key questions for innovators)

Acknowledgements

When I reflect on the journey to craft this book, I can only give complete honor and glory to God. He laid the vision and provided the inspiration, resources, physical and emotional strength and links required to complete it. I would like to recognize the publisher – Routledge, and especially Tim Hardwick. I would also like to thank the M-RCBG at the Harvard Kennedy School for the opportunity to serve as a Senior Fellow, and to recognize Jennifer Nash, the amazing faculty and other senior fellows, who provided tremendous advice and support. Prof. Calestous Juma, my faculty sponsor provided terrific encouragement and the link to Routledge. I would like to thank Prof. Debora Spar and Prof. Lisa Cook, two great friends and mentors who recommended the Kennedy School in the first place. A special thank you to my dear mentor and friend – Dr. Pamela Hartigan – for providing links to social innovators, critically reviewing the book and serving as a source of inspiration and encouragement during my journey as a social entrepreneur. Thank you to Prof. Linda Hill, another amazing mentor and role model, Harvard Business School's Initiative on Social Enterprise, and the great reservoir of knowledge in Boston provided by Heiner Baumann, Jeff Bradach, Margot Dushin, Marcela Escobari, Willie Foot, Allan Grossman, Jane Nelson, Jacob Olupona, Nan Stone and David Wilcox.

I would like to acknowledge the amazing social innovators, facilitators, funders, policy makers and impact investors who spent hours with me over the telephone, in face-to-face meetings and via email exchanges, providing insights and feedback. Many of them are profiled and quoted in this book, and their work is truly inspirational. The organizations include: Action Health Inc., Acumen Fund, Aflatoun, Allied Crowds, ANDE, Ashoka and Ashoka Fellows across Africa, Bertha Center for Social Innovation & Entrepreneurship of the University of Cape Town, Bridge International Academies, Brookings Institute, Center for Education Innovations, Chemonics, Co-Creation Hub, Dalberg, Dimagi, DEEPEN, Draper Richards Kaplan Foundation, Echoing Green Foundation, Educate!, ESSPIN, Ford Foundation, FSG, GADCO, GAIN, GIIN, Global Fund for Women, ICSF, IFAD, IFDC, Ikamva Youth, Innovations for Gender Equality Program, Jacaranda, Jobberman, Kenya Feed the Future Innovation Engine (KFIE), Kidogo, MacArthur Foundation, Mercy Corps, Millions Learn, LYNX, MIT D-Lab, Moringaconnect, mPedigree, MSI, Off-Grid

Electric, Omidyar, One Acre Fund, PIN, R4D, Riders for Health, Root Capital, Sanergy, Slum2School, Social Finance, Social Franchising Accelerator, Sproxil, Technoserve, Teso Women Development Initiatives, The Bill & Melinda Gates Foundation, The Skoll Foundation, USAID, Village Capital, Volans, and WAVE.

A special thank you to Johannes Linn – a truly remarkable man who is an authority on scaling – Isabel Guerrero, Francois Bonnici, Bill Carter, Kole Shettima, who provided advice, encouragement, insights and linkages through this process. Also thanks to Chinezi & Eric Chijoke, Chris Dede, Olivia Leland, Kelechi Ohiri, Nana Tum-Danso, Kandeh Yumkellah, Georgia Levenson Keohane, and Paul Bloom.

I would like to thank Nanre Nafzinger-Mayegun for serving as a fantastic thought partner and providing critical feedback from the social entrepreneur's lens, my Godmother – Rebecca Nwude, for engaging in the painful editing process, and being so thorough and thoughtful, Jade Adeniji, Nadu Denloye, Orode Doherty, Ngozi Enelamah, Eme Essien, Uzoma Ezeoke, Toyosi Kolawole, Nneka Mobisson-Etuk, Oge Modie, Nwamaka Nwobi, Adaobi Nwaubani, Jumoke Oduwole, Nkiru Okpareke, Shivam Mallick-Shah – my spiritual sisters. Thank you to my volunteers including Akwugo Nnama, Alicia Bello, Falaq Tidjani, Hectoria Mills-Roberton Asuquo, Emeka Ilukwe, Olusola Adeola, Rhode Ahlonsou, Temi Adegoroye, Uche Okonkwo, Uzoma Ikechukwu, Yemi Onafuye, and Yewande Adefarasin, who supported my research and editing efforts. Thank you – the AACE Foods, LEAP Africa and Sahel Capital families who provided the experiences, the space and the understanding that I required to engage in this activity, as I attempted to juggle my multiple responsibilities, often dropping a few balls.

Thank you to my earliest professional mentors who nurtured my interest in social entrepreneurship including Bernard Loyd, Jill Stever, Andrea Silbert, Adhiambo Odaga and Fola Adeola.

I would like to acknowledge the invaluable role provided by my mother – Prof. Rina Okonkwo whose guidance and editing support was invaluable, my father – Prof. Paul Okonkwo, my sisters – Adaora, Nwando, and Una and my brother – Aneto – all God's special gift to me. Finally, my husband – Mezuo Nwuneli for his encouragement and my children – Amara and Udenna – who provided the needed distractions, challenged my time management skills and provided the impetus for the book – a deep desire for a brighter future for them and countless other African children and generations yet unborn.

Foreword

When Ndidi started this journey to write a book on social innovation in Africa, I was delighted – at last a strong African voice to speak from the continent.

Ndidi and I had met in 2005, while working with the Schwab Foundation and World Economic Forum uncovering social entrepreneurs in Africa. For over a decade, I've admirably followed her pioneering work. Ndidi has been an inspiration to a generation of social innovators in Nigeria, and a role model to many others across the African continent.

With our 54 countries, our estimated 2,000 languages and our billion people – our continent is filled with beautiful diversity and heterogeneity. It's also mind-numbingly vast in size: Kai Krause's astonishing geographic visualisation of the *True Size of Africa*[1] illustrates how it contains the entirety of the USA, all of China, India and Japan, as well as most of Europe, all combined.

Our continent is rich with possibility, not only filled with challenges and problems to be fixed, but it is a continent that is still shaping its own future. While we have a great need for governance, leadership and macro-economic stewardship, we urgently also need the voices and ideas of citizens and social sector actors to rise up and meet the top-down policies.

We have the opportunity to follow new pathways to development, not only using those strategies of the multilateral and international agencies, but also to evolve home-grown strategies that are inclusive of the voice and needs of local citizens. We therefore need the social innovations that are shown to be effective in accelerating social impact and social justice to be scaled higher, further and deeper, and work both in parallel in the private sector, but also integrating with our governments to do so.

When Ndidi began researching this book, we spoke at length of the many social entrepreneurs and innovations across the continent that collectively we had encountered or knew of – and many more that we knew were under the radar and newly emerging. But after 10 years it was clear that there were only a handful of these that had significantly scaled their impact or shifted their sectors towards more systemic change.

Rather than dwell on the barriers only, or tell a story of a few hard-to-replicate successes, this book concentrates on what could practically and immediately support scaling our local social innovations – by understanding the ecosystem and resources available on and to the continent.

If you're advancing social innovation in your communities, your organization, your sectors or your country, this book presents a comprehensive review of the frameworks of thinking, the key pieces of the puzzle, and, through a rich journey of interviews, unpacks insights into some fascinating cases on the continent.

Ndidi's path continues to be one of action, and through that, an inspiration to others in Africa – and now her gift to us all is a guide to make our own paths wider, to make them go further, intersecting with others as we join her call.

Dr François Bonnici
Director
Bertha Centre for Social Innovation and Entrepreneurship
Graduate School of Business
University of Cape Town

Note

1   *The True Size of Africa*, Kai Krause, http://kai.sub.blue/en/africa.html

Introduction

As a serial social entrepreneur, I define success as the day when the innovations that I have launched or supported over the past 15 years have transformed the social landscapes which they were set out to change. Furthermore, the innovations would have become credible frameworks being implemented across and beyond the African continent. The organizations that manage these innovations would have achieved their initial objectives and dramatically changed their strategies to tackle new problems because the gap that they were initially created to fill would be closed. In my dreams of success,

- LEAP Africa, which is committed to inspiring, empowering and equipping a new cadre of African leaders by providing the skills and tools for personal, organizational and community transformation, would be celebrating the successful adoption of its Leadership, Ethics & Civics (LEC) curriculum by the Nigerian government as part of its core teacher training program and high school curricula. This would ensure that millions of youth benefit from life and leadership skills which would enable them to make positive changes in their communities, and empower them to enroll in higher education, get better jobs and start businesses. The government would engage independent and credible third parties to evaluate the impact of the national LEC program, via mindset surveys which would demonstrate that Nigerian youth are becoming more ethical, principled and dynamic and that millions of change projects have been implemented by them to improve the lives of others in their communities.
- Ndu Ike Akunuba (NIA), which empowers female university students in the Southeastern part of Nigeria to achieve their highest potential, would have shifted the focus of its activities to new challenges because the leadership and economic gap between young women and their male counterparts would be closed. This would have been achieved through a concerted effort by multiple stakeholders to develop and sustain local, state and national policies and programs which have successfully created a level playing field for all genders.
- AACE Food Processing & Distribution Ltd. would be celebrating a five percent rate of stunting in Nigerian children under five years of age as opposed to 37 percent in 2013. This dramatic decline would be primarily linked to

AACE Foods providing Soyamaize and Soso Nourish products and partnering with other manufacturers of high-energy foods and international nonprofits to fight malnutrition in Nigeria.

In reality, my dreams of working myself and others out of a job seem distant. LEAP, NIA and AACE Foods, established between 2002 and 2010, have experienced some moderate impact at tackling the serious social challenges for which they were established. However, their ability to achieve the picture of true success outlined in these brief descriptions seems impossible in my lifetime.

The sad reality is that many other social entrepreneurs and innovators operating in the private, public and nonprofit sectors share my frustrations about the slow and arduous pace of social change on the African continent. Like me, they often feel like they are working tirelessly to solve deep-rooted problems in their communities, countries and regions, but are barely moving the needle. *Scaling their impact* – transforming the lives of millions of people, instead of only hundreds or thousands, changing mindsets and ideologies, shaping ecosystems and policies, often seems an elusive goal.

The quest to uncover why countless social innovations operating on the African continent are struggling to *scale impact* led me to enroll in the Mossavar-Rahmani Center for Business & Government at the Harvard Kennedy School as a Senior Fellow. Through this program, I have had the unique privilege of engaging in robust conversations with over 80 social entrepreneurs across Africa and with a range of stakeholders who support them, including development partners, impact investors, research organizations, government agencies and the private sector. These broad-based consultations revealed four truths:

1 **The scaling challenge is shared by social entrepreneurs across the globe; but Africa has some unique challenges.** Social innovators and impact investors interviewed for this book argue that scaling is tough on the African continent, only comparable to South Asia. Anecdotal evidence suggests that there are at least four key drivers of these unique scaling difficulties. First, the lack of credible data for local communities, countries and regions slows down the processes for planning, piloting and scaling social innovations and hinders the ability of key stakeholders to measure their impact on society. Second, the heterogeneity within and across countries, which includes significant diversity in colonial histories, language, religion, culture, community assets, and social development, essentially means that there is 'no single story'. Innovations have to be tweaked or significantly altered to enable scaling from one community to another, which is not only more expensive, but also slows the scaling process. Thirdly, the fragmented ecosystems, in almost every sector, especially the agricultural, education and health landscapes, limit the ability of innovators to reach large numbers of people in record time. Consider the agriculture sector, where 85 percent of arable land in Africa is cultivated by farmers with less than 2 hectares. This essentially means that any intervention that wants to scale in this sector can

only do so by working with farmer clusters as opposed to individual farmers. The process of creating clusters of farmers, hospitals, schools, small and medium-sized enterprises, and other sectors and building trust among these groups takes time and requires financial resources. Fourth, there are significant talent, infrastructure and financing gaps which limit scaling. According to the World Bank,[1] 48 countries of Sub-Saharan Africa generate approximately the same amount of power as Spain. This significant power deficit has limited technology innovations that require electricity, spurring the emergence of off-grid solutions. In addition, 'only one-third of Africans living in rural areas are within two kilometers of an all-season road, compared with two-thirds of the population in other developing regions'.[2] This in turn makes it extremely difficult and expensive to extend healthcare, education, and agriculture innovations to communities in rural areas. Sadly, with underdeveloped distribution and marketing systems, social innovators essentially have to work along all aspects of the value chain, filling gaps that ordinarily would not exist in other markets to reach people.

Clearly in spite of these difficulties, there is a real sense of urgency to scaling high-impact social innovations on the African continent. As highlighted in a recent World Bank article,

> In 1990, East Asia accounted for half of the global poor, whereas some 15 percent lived in Sub-Saharan Africa; by 2015 forecasts, this is almost exactly reversed: Sub-Saharan Africa accounts for half of the global poor, with some 12 percent living in East Asia…The growing concentration of global poverty in Sub-Saharan Africa is of great concern. While some African countries have seen significant successes in reducing poverty, the region as a whole lags behind the rest of the world in the pace of lessening poverty.[3]

UNICEF estimates Africa's population will reach 2.4 billion by 2050. With over 70 percent of the population under 30 years old, and over 60 percent in urban areas, there is a heightened need for more scalable, high-impact innovations in the education, healthcare, agriculture, energy, housing, environment and transportation sectors.

2   **Not all social innovations can or should be scaled.** Some innovations should be discarded because they are not demand-driven or scalable, and a few social innovation initiatives should remain relatively small and serve as centers of excellence for others to emulate, which in itself can be considered a form of scaling processes, ideas and methodologies. For example, the widely celebrated Ashesi University, established by Ghanaian Patrick Awuah, has made a conscious decision to remain a center of excellence on the continent. With a student body size of under 700, Ashesi is focused on delivering its mission,[4] 'to educate a new generation of ethical and entrepreneurial leaders in Africa; to cultivate within our students the critical thinking skills, the concern for others and the courage it will take to transform their continent'.

Its results over the past 13 years demonstrate its impact: 100 percent of its graduates have received job offers, started their own businesses or gone on to pursue postgraduate degrees in top universities around the world – within months of graduation. Over 90 percent of the alumni live and work in Africa, helping expand businesses, influencing society and committed to helping create a renaissance across Africa.

3 **There is no straight line to scale**. It is typically an iterative and interactive process. Indeed, the insights gained from failed attempts at scaling successful pilots are an integral component of the learning and innovation process.

4 **It is possible to scale social innovations in Africa**. However, for success, scaling has to be embedded into the initiative's mission, vision, values and operating strategy. The organization which 'hosts the innovation' has to design an appropriate business model with human resource management and financing strategies that enable scaling. In addition, it has to develop the capacity to build strong cross-sector partnerships, with the private sector, governments, and civil society and shape environments in which it operates.

This book focuses exclusively on the fourth truth and delves into the steps required to scale impact on the African continent from the perspective of those who are doing it. It utilizes the definition of social innovation provided by the Stanford Social Innovation Review (SSIR)[5] which recognizes a social innovation as a novel solution to a social problem where the value created accrues primarily to society. Novel can refer either to a completely original idea or an old idea applied in a new sector – which can be a product, production process, technology, a principle, an idea, a piece of legislation, a social movement, an intervention, or some combination of them. Social problems are defined as challenges where the majority of the benefit accrues to society or disadvantaged groups rather than to individuals.

In the context of social innovation, scale is the ability to extend the impact of an innovation to enhance the lives of large numbers of people. This meaning and its application varies based on what is being scaled and for what purpose, as will be outlined in subsequent chapters.

It is important to note that this book is largely focused on Sub-Saharan Africa, and the vast majority of the case studies are from East and West Africa.

I have been personally inspired and challenged by the ability of many courageous social innovators and their team members to scale impact in Africa. All three organizations in which I am actively involved are already benefiting from the knowledge and the insights that I have gained from this process.

I am confident that you, your team and key stakeholders engaged in the development process in Africa will benefit immensely from reading this book. It is my hope that it will serve as a catalyst for social change on the African continent – in our life-time – making Africa significantly better for our children and generations yet unborn.

Notes

1   Fact Sheet: Infrastructure in Sub-Saharan Africa; http://web.worldbank.org/
     WBSITE/EXTERNAL/COUNTRIES/AFRICAEXT/0,,contentMDK:21951811~page
     PK:146736~piPK:146830~theSitePK:258644,00.html
2   Ibid.
3   'World Bank forecasts global poverty to fall below 10 percent for first time; major
     hurdles remain in goal to end poverty by 2030', October 4, 2015; www.world
     bank.org/en/news/press-release/2015/10/04/world-bank-forecasts-global-poverty-to-
     fall-below-10-for-first-time-major-hurdles-remain-in-goal-to-end-poverty-by-2030
4   Ashesi website, accessed October 30, 2015; www.ashesi.edu.gh/about/ashesi-at-a-
     glance/mission-history.html
5   Phillis James, Deiglmeier Kriss, Miller Dale, 'Rediscovering social innovation',
     Stanford Social Innovation Review, Fall 2008; http://ssir.org/articles/entry/
     rediscovering_social_innovation/#sthash.rzN44R4j.dpufhttp://www.ssireview.org/
     articles/entry/rediscovering_social_innovation/

1 Vision for scale

Scaling solutions to the world's social and economic problems is already astonishingly difficult. Yet nonprofits, funders, and social ventures make it even harder by falling prey to stifling incrementalism, where 'success' is measured just a few marginal increments from the status quo—often still light years from really solving our problems. This positioning quashes real innovation by never aiming high enough and ultimately leads to rationalized mediocrity. We set the bar lower and lower because the problems are hard, and we often declare success despite the fact that our impact is embarrassingly small compared to the size of the problems we are trying to solve.[1]

(Ben Mangan, a social entrepreneur, Executive Director of the Center for Social Sector Leadership and Lecturer at Haas Berkeley)

Introduction

In the development landscape, the concept of 'small is beautiful' has often been held up as the ideal. Clearly, Africa's future cannot be hinged on this premise as there is a real sense of urgency for change, driven by demographic, environmental and social trends. How can this continent possibly feed, educate, house, and provide health care, energy, sanitation and transportation for 2.4 billion people by 2050, when it struggles to meet the needs of 900 million people today? Indeed, the depth and breadth of the needs in Sub-Saharan Africa deserve bold attempts at scaling what works.

This chapter lays out the critical building blocks for scaling which are universal but amplified by the examples of social innovators on the continent. Their experiences reinforce that social innovators clearly need to define their vision for social change and outline what success looks like. This vision has to be anchored in a clear mission and values which set the boundaries required for focus and intensity. The structure of the intervention and the selected pathways for scale provide the medium through which the social innovator builds a compelling business model, a clear talent and financing strategy and identifies strategic partnerships to enable scaling.

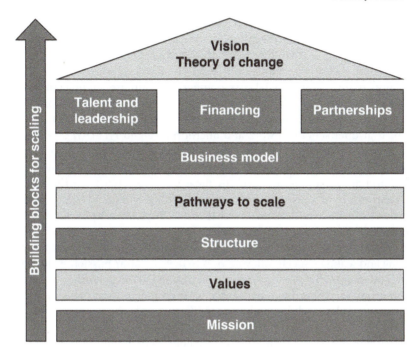

Figure 1.1 Building blocks for scaling social innovation
Source: Developed by Ndidi Okonkwo Nwuneli.

This chapter focuses on the vision, mission, values, structure and pathways for scaling, leveraging examples from the African context. Subsequent chapters focus on the other components of the model.

Mission, values and vision

As social innovators work diligently to pilot, roll-out and scale impact, one of the easiest traps that many fall into, especially in the African context, is the loss of focus. This is often driven by two issues. First, the more one delves into a social problem, the more needs he or she discovers. The depth and breadth of social problems often overwhelms the innovator. Focusing on a predefined set of needs requires discipline.

Consider the innovations identified by the Innovation Countdown 2030 in their publication titled, 'Reimagining global health: 30 high-impact innovations to save lives.'[2] The list of interventions includes the uterine balloon tamponade – a low-cost kit to manage postpartum hemorrhage, which could potentially save 169,000 lives for $29 million. Another innovation is the use of chlorhexidine for umbilical cord care, which can save over 1 million babies for $81 million. There is also the portable Phone Oximeter which improves pneumonia detection and can save 772,000 children for $101 million. These interventions look very promising and the innovations linked to the largest numbers to be saved look even more attractive. Which intervention would you focus on if you were a social innovator working to save lives especially in the area of maternal and infant health? There is clearly a temptation to work on all innovations.

Second, many credible social entrepreneurs face intense funding challenges and pressure from society which compels them to tackle more social problems than they can adequately handle. It is not uncommon to find nonprofit organizations that offer school to work and microfinance and HIV/AIDs programs, all under the same roof, simply because a funder has offered to support such projects. Sadly, many of these social enterprises quickly become a 'jack of all trades' and are unable to achieve any measure of excellence in their social interventions. In addition, they gradually drift from their social change agenda and eventually become contractors or program implementers for funders and other stakeholders.

A critical first step to staying focused, especially in the early days of implementing and scaling a social innovation, is to develop **clear mission, values and vision statements.** These terms are often confused with each other and many organizations use them interchangeably or even merge them. However, it is important to understand that each term is different and important.

- A **mission statement** expresses the core purpose of an entity, clearly stating why it exists and setting clear boundaries around its key activities.
- **Values** define the enduring character of the entity, outlining key principles that are critical to the organization's existence, which it is unwilling to compromise.
- A **vision statement** provides a glimpse of success – the future desired state of achievement that the innovator and his or her team are working to achieve.

For example, South Africa's Ikamva Youth's[3] mission is to enable disadvantaged youth to pull themselves and each other out of poverty and into tertiary education and/or employment.

Its five explicitly stated values are:
- a culture of responsibility for self and others
- collaboration and peer-to-peer support
- commitment to impact through democratic processes
- integrity and openness
- paying-it-forward.

Its vision statement states – 'Our culture of responsibility is creating a ripple effect of thriving individuals and communities. Our intergenerational ikamvanites provide access to quality education in inspirational spaces everywhere. We are an integrated network driving change by paying it forward.'

These three statements guide every aspect of Ikamva Youth's operations and keep the team focused. For example, the explicitly stated value – 'paying-it-forward' is an integral component of Ikamva's business model. According to Joy Olivier, the co-founder and director of the organization, 'Learners who benefit from the program become tutors and some even become employees of Ikamva.'

East Africa's One Acre Fund[4] has defined its purpose as follows: 'We serve small-scale farmers. In everything we do, we place the farmer first. We measure success in our ability to make more farmers more prosperous.'

Its six values:
- Humble service: we meet farmers in their fields, and we get our shoes muddy. Farmers are our customers, and we serve them with humility.
- Hard work: we work hard every day. We execute with world-class professionalism and business excellence. Farmers deserve nothing less.
- Continual growth: we improve every season. We work with determination to meet our goals and then stretch ourselves by raising the bar even higher.
- Family of leaders: we bring together the best leaders and build long-term careers. We care for team members like family.
- Dreaming big: we envision serving millions of farm families. We build for scale with every idea and solution.
- Integrity: we do what we say, and our words match our values.

An excerpt from One Acre Fund's vision statement[5] clearly outlines the organization's image of success. It states that, 'by 2020, we will serve at least 1 million farm families – with more than 5 million people living in those families. And our farmers will produce enough surplus food to feed another 5 million of their neighbors. This is only the tip of the iceberg. When millions of farmers speak with one voice, we can more effectively pursue collaboration together with government and the private sector to broaden our reach.'

The mission, values and vision articulated by One Acre are focused on meeting the needs of farmers and enabling them to improve their productivity and livelihoods. In addition, scale is a critical aspect of the organization's values, and is clearly incorporated into its vision statement.

Kidogo,[6] based in Kenya, which provides high-quality, affordable early childhood care and education for less than $1 per day, has an explicit mission statement: 'Through our growing network of daycares and pre-schools, we seek to unlock the potential of young children, empower mama-preneurs, and transform the trajectory of families living in informal settlements.'

Kidogo's five explicitly stated values are:
- **Curious:** we approach our work with wide-eyed optimism, a willingness to experiment, learn, take risks and challenge the status quo. We innovate by listening and observing, and combine global best practices with local realities.
- **Playful:** play is the brain's favorite way to learn, and it's our favorite way to lead. We are light-hearted, have a sense of humor, and enjoy having fun. We take our work seriously, but not ourselves. Also, we like naps.

- **Bold:** we don't settle for mediocrity... we are literally the elephant in the room. We set big, hairy, ambitious goals and relentlessly measure our impact to ensure we are making a meaningful dent in the world.
- **Resourceful:** our programs aim to be financially sustainable, community-driven and culturally appropriate. We aim to do more with less. We don't compromise on quality. We leverage partnerships and find better ways to collaborate to get things done.
- **Transparent:** we try to set a good example for our students. We don't pay bribes and we don't tolerate corruption. We strive for excellence but are not afraid to admit and learn from our mistakes.

Kidogo's vision is a world in which every child has the opportunity to reach their full potential regardless of where they were born.

According to Kevin Star,[7] of Mulago Foundation and the Rainer Arnold Fellows Program, who supports a number of social innovators on the African continent,

> Razor-sharp clarity about where you're going allows you to ask three critically important questions: 1) Is this the best way to get there? 2) Is there anything else we should be doing to accelerate along the path? and 3) Is everything we're doing really focused on getting there? The first question helps prevent the bane of startups, fixing too early and rigidly on a specific idea; the second pushes evolution of models and activities; and the third helps you avoid or get rid of stuff that is a distraction or waste of bandwidth.

Mr. Star even advocates for mission statements that are restricted to eight words, to push organizations to narrow their focus.

BOX 1.1: KEY QUESTIONS FOR INNOVATORS

Clarifying your vision, mission and values

- What problem in society are you trying to address?
- What innovation have you conceived to address the problem?
- Which groups of people are you targeting with this innovation?
- Which entity is best positioned to pilot and/or scale this innovation (note that some innovations can be incubated and tested by one entity, but may be better scaled by others)?

Mission-specific questions:
- Why does your innovation exist?
- What is its core purpose?
- How will it achieve this core purpose?

Values-specific questions:
- What principles are critical for success? What principles are you unwilling to compromise with growth in reach and impact?

Vision-specific questions:
- What is your definition of a successful pilot?
- What is your definition of success at scale?
- How will you know that you have arrived at your destination?

Beyond clearly articulating and communicating the mission, values and vision statements, social innovators have to ensure these words serve as effective guiding principles for their team members and key stakeholders. They are extremely critical during periods of growth or contraction, because they enable the team to remain focused in the face of internal or external pressure.

Theory of change

A **theory of change** is defined as the assumptions and building blocks required to achieve a given long-term goal. Though the process of developing a 'theory of change' is a difficult and time-consuming undertaking, it is critical for every social innovator. It compels the innovator to engage a broad range of critical stakeholders to determine the inputs, activities, outputs, and outcomes required for a social innovation.

Consider the case of Sanergy, a social enterprise focused on addressing the sanitation challenges in Africa's urban informal settlements using a systems-based approach. Its vision is to build healthy, prosperous communities by making hygienic sanitation accessible and affordable for everyone, forever. In order to achieve these results, its operations have three pillars:

- a dense network of micro-franchised small-scale sanitation centers, known as 'fresh life toilets', located throughout informal settlements
- a containerized collection infrastructure to easily transport the waste out of the community
- a centralized processing facility that efficiently converts the waste into high-quality organic fertilizer and other by-products, which are sold to regional farmers.

The theory of change which guides its activities is articulated in Table 1. Sanergy's theory of change has been instrumental to its early successes, enabling the organization to rally internal and external support for achieving its short, medium and long term goals.

Table 1.1 Theory of change for Sanergy

What is the problem you are trying to solve?	Who is the key audience?	What steps are needed to bring about change?	What is the measurable effect of your work?	What are the wider benefits of your work?	What is the long-term change you see as your goal?
Sanitation challenge Kenya's 8 million slum residents are forced to rely on unsanitary options such as 'flying toilets' (defecating into plastic bags that are then tossed onto the streets) and pit latrines that release untreated human waste into the environment. These sanitation solutions are not only undignified, but also cause immense environmental damage. Pit latrines are emptied every few months by poorly trained and equipped service employees. These 'frogmen' jump into the pits of human waste, manually empty the pit latrines using buckets, and then haul the overflowing buckets of waste through the community to the nearest waterway or field, where the buckets' contents are released into the environment. In total, 4 million tons — or 90 percent — of fecal sludge from Kenya's slums are	Sanergy's key audiences are residents of urban informal settlements who currently lack access to hygienic sanitation options and farmers looking to restore their soil health and increase their crop yields. Sanergy serves the most at-risk populations, namely women and children.	User education is a fundamental part of building healthy, prosperous communities. Sanergy works to educate customers and potential customers on the implications of unhygienic toilets and the importance of choosing a hygienic alternative. Sanergy currently has three different distribution models for its toilets: a commercial model, a residential model, and a community model. Sanergy's commercial	Since November 2011, Sanergy has established 734 fresh life toilets run by 362 fresh life operators in 8 informal settlements around Nairobi. Sanergy's network is used more than 33,000 times per day, and Sanergy removes more than 7 tons of waste from the community each day. In total, Sanergy has removed and treated more than 6,000 tons of waste. Sanergy has created more than 760 jobs. Sanergy's main	By removing waste from toilets on a daily basis, Sanergy cleans up the community as a whole. By properly treating the waste, Sanergy reduces waste-related pollution of major waterways. In addition, through education initiatives, Sanergy is teaching people – fresh life users and non-users – about proper hygiene practices, so that they can lead healthier lives.	Build healthy, prosperous communities by making hygienic sanitation affordable and accessible for everyone, forever.

Table 1.1 Continued.

What is the problem you are trying to solve?	Who is the key audience?	What steps are needed to bring about change?	What is the measurable effect of your work?	What are the wider benefits of your work?	What is the long-term change you see as your goal?
discharged into waterways and fields every year. **Agriculture challenge** 80 percent of Kenyans rely on agriculture for their livelihoods, but farmers are often stuck in a poverty trap due to declining agricultural productivity. Without enough nutrients and organic material being restored into the soil, each harvest further depletes the land, and farmers are trapped in a downward spiral of declining soil fertility and decreasing yields. The Kenyan Ministry of Agriculture has identified soil degradation as the number one issue surrounding Kenya's food security. As such, the Ministry of Agriculture has recommended that farmers use up to 10 tons of organic fertilizer per hectare to restore soil health.		distribution model is well established, but Sanergy is working on refining its residential and community distribution models, so as to achieve 100 percent coverage in the communities.	byproduct, Evergrow Fertilizer, improves soil health and increases crop yields 30–100 percent.		

Table 1.1 Continued.

What is the problem you are trying to solve?	Who is the key audience?	What steps are needed to bring about change?	What is the measurable effect of your work?	What are the wider benefits of your work?	What is the long-term change you see as your goal?
However, regional farmers do not have ready access to organic fertilizers, as they are not produced domestically, and imports are prohibitively expensive.					
Key assumptions: People who lack access to hygienic sanitation want and would use a sanitation option that is hygienic, accessible, and affordable. There is a market for domestically produced organic fertilizer for East African farms.	**Key assumptions:** Residents will use a hygienic sanitation alternative, once they are educated about the importance of proper hygiene practices. Farmers will change their current practices and suppliers if they believe it will increase their profits.	**Key assumptions:** User education on the importance of good hygiene and how best to practice it will lead to behavior change.	NA	NA	NA

Source: Interviews with the Sanergy team for this publication.

Structure

In addition to developing and imbibing clear visions, missions and values, social innovators need to determine the most appropriate structure to operationalize the innovation. They can choose to establish entities in the public, private and nonprofit sectors, or even hybrids, based on which option best aligns with their mission and vision.

Nonprofit

Social innovators who select this model believe that their venture will require subsidies for an extended period of time or even for the lifetime of the inter-vention. This is often because the ideology, product, or service that is being offered has limited income-generating potential in the short-term. It often targets people at the bottom of the pyramid, who ultimately cannot pay market rates and need subsidies in order to realize the benefits. These entities obtain donations from individuals, foundations, and corporations, who expect a 'social return on their investment,' often referred to as SROI. Nonprofits are often referred to as Non-governmental organizations (NGOs) or civil society organizations (CSOs).

> **Example: LEAP Africa**, an organization committed to inspiring, empowering and equipping a new cadre of African leaders, is structured as a nonprofit. While it generates earned income through program fees and book sales, this only covers 36 percent of its operating expenses. The balance is obtained by grants and donations, primarily because the teachers and youth who LEAP serves with its Youth Development Training Program and School to Work Program, respec-tively, cannot afford to pay for the training and coaching services they receive. To date, LEAP has trained over 45,000 Nigerians through its core programs, and its beneficiaries have created over 1,000 change projects in their communities, transforming the lives of over 250,000 people.

For-profit

Social innovators who select this model believe that their venture will ultimately be able to break-even and generate profits. They can raise money from private investors and financial institutions and must give some confidence of a profitable exit and timely repayments for the investors. They can also benefit from finite, small grants to support the testing and scaling of aspects of their business model specifically focused on social change. For-profits with a social mission are often referred to as social ventures or social businesses.

> **Example: AACE Food Processing & Distribution Ltd.**, a private company which operates in Nigeria, is an example of a for-profit organization, which from the onset was conceived as a social enterprise. AACE sources grains, herbs, cereals and vegetables from smallholder farmers in Nigeria and

produces a range of spices, spreads and complementary food for retail and institutional buyers. It is also focused on addressing the high rates of malnutrition in Nigeria and improving the livelihoods of smallholder farmers by offering microfinance, training, and support services to them. To date, AACE has raised funds from its founders and private investors. It has benefited from funding from the Africa Diaspora Marketplace Competition, the African Enterprise Challenge Fund and Innovations against Poverty which enabled AACE to cover a portion of its start-up and farmer cluster development and training costs, and new product innovation.

Among large corporations, social innovations developed by employees or adopted via acquisition or partnerships are embedded within the core operations of the company or within a subsidiary. The company typically utilizes its funds to pilot and roll-out the innovation and occasionally benefits from external funding from development partners and foundations.

Example: Safaricom's M-Pesa is the classic example of a social innovation within a large corporation. Funding from United Kingdom's Department for International Development (DFID) enabled Safaricom – one of the leading mobile phone providers in East Africa – to test and launch a new, mobile phone-based payment and money transfer service. Safaricom leveraged the innovation and its infrastructure to develop a set of new products, and supporting and related structures. By 2015, M-Pesa had reached 19.6 million people – over 70 percent of households in Kenya and over 50 percent of the poor, unbanked and rural populations.

Hybrid

Social innovators who select this model can distinguish between components of their operations that require subsidies in the medium-long term and components that are not only self-sustaining, but ultimately profitable. A growing number of social innovators in Africa have both a nonprofit and a for-profit, either as a subsidiary of one another or two independent entities. This allows them to benefit from the funding sources available to both a nonprofit and a for-profit. Some innovators have incorporated for-profits on the African continent, and also manage sister nonprofit organizations in the United States to drive the related fundraising efforts required to generate support or vice versa.

Example: Bridge International Academies, a low-cost provider of quality education which operates a chain of schools for the urban poor in Kenya, has a for-profit company registered in Kenya and a nonprofit registered as a 501(c)3 in the United States. Similarly, Jacaranda Health, an innovative provider of maternal healthcare services, has a registered for-profit enterprise in Kenya, which is a subsidiary of a nonprofit registered in the United States. These ventures focus on different aspects of the same problem and enable the entity to raise grants, via the nonprofit and venture funding via the social business venture.

Public sector

Social innovations developed by government employees or adopted from social innovators are embedded within the core operations of the relevant government ministry, agency or parastatal or within a new entity – established for the sole purpose of implementing the innovation. The government typically utilizes its own resources or funding from development partners and foundations to pilot and scale the innovation, eventually taking on full financial responsibility for the scaling and sustainability efforts.

> **Example: The Ethiopia Commodity Exchange (ECX),** operates as a stand-alone entity, with the Ministry of Agriculture providing key oversight. It was initiated in 2008 as a platform to facilitate agricultural produce trade between buyers and sellers and to protect both farmers and traders from price drops and price hikes. ECX provides transparent price information for both farmers and buyers, harnesses technology and storage infrastructure to mobilize products from smallholder farmers and ensures product quality, delivery, and payment. ECX initially focused on coffee, sesame, haricot beans, maize and wheat. As of July 2014, 2.5 million tons of commodities, worth 96.7 billion Birr (4.7 billion USD) had been traded through ECX, catering to 2.7 million smallholder farmers.

Ultimately, each social innovator needs to determine which operating structure is most ideal to enable their entity to thrive and scale impact.

Table 1.2 Selecting an appropriate structure: guide for social innovators

Structure	Nonprofit	For-profit	Hybrid
Description	Incorporate a nonprofit limited by guarantee or via articles of association	Incorporate a limited liability company or a partnership with shareholders	Incorporate two entities: a nonprofit and a for profit, either as distinct organizations or one as a subsidiary of another
Best suited for?	Innovations that will need grants or subsidies in the long-term given the nature of the innovation and/or its target beneficiaries	Innovations that will eventually break even and generate profits for shareholders and investors. Viable exit path for investors	Innovations that have components that require subsidies and others that can generate profit

Source: Developed by Ndidi Nwuneli.

B-Corps

It is important to recognize that there are emerging classifications for social enterprises that choose to reinvest all of their profits into a social cause or meet specific environmental and social impact standards. More specifically, there are enterprises being certified by the B Lab, a nonprofit in the United States which was established in 2006 as B-Corps. The B Lab utilizes an assessment tool to evaluate the impact of a company on its key stakeholders – its workers, suppliers, community, and the environment. It also considers the organization's business model and its impact on particular stakeholders through its products and services or internal practices. Companies must score at least 80 points[9] on the B Impact Assessment to have achieved a significant threshold of impact.

As of September 2015,[10] there were over 1,395 certified B Corporations across 130 industries in 42 countries. On the African continent, there are 9 companies recognized as B-Corps. They include Zoona, a mobile money operator based in South Africa and the Open University of West Africa registered in Ghana. Five B-Corps operate in Kenya – the Charleston Travel Limited which provides travel management services, EcoZoom Designs, which manufacturers and distributes high-efficiency cookstoves, Juhudi Kilimo, which provides asset financing for rural smallholder farmers, ECO2LIBRIUM which applies business solutions to solve social and environmental problems and Daproim Africa, an outsourcing social enterprise that offers data management services. Tanzania has two B-Corps – Asilia Africa Ltd which operates camps, lodges and safaris and Opulent Group which is a property developer and operator.

Pathways to scaling

Social innovators have to determine the most appropriate pathway to scale their social innovations, hinged on their theory of change, mission and values. There are numerous models, with overlaps, that have been developed by authorities in the social sector which serve as useful tools for innovators. Three key models which have influenced this book are outlined below:

Larry Cooley and Richard Kohl of Management Systems International (MSI) in their publication *Scaling Up: From Vision to Large-scale Change*,[11] identify three types and methods of scaling up – expansion, replication and collaborations. Under expansion – growth, restructuring or decentralization, – franchising and spin-offs were identified as the key approaches. Replication occurs through policy adoption, grafting (where a model or component of a model is incorporated into another organization's services or delivery mechanism), diffusion and spillover and mass media. Under collaborations, scaling occurs through formal partnerships, joint ventures, strategic alliances or networks, and coalitions.

The second model proposed by Julia Coffman, as part of the Harvard Family Research Project in 2010, outlines four[12] approaches to scaling based on exactly what is being scaled. For products or services, scaling is defined as expansion, replication and adaptation to new areas or populations, or the deepening of an already-served area. For ideologies and methodologies, scaling is defined as

Table 1.3 Four approaches to scale

What is scaled	Definition of scale	Scaling mechanisms
Program		
A system of projects or services that meets a need for individuals or communities	Copying a program that research has shown to be effective, with the expectation that it can or will produce the same results in different places. Scales programs often allow for flexibility in implementation to best adapt to the local context	Replication Adaptation
Idea or innovation		
A new way of thinking about or doing something; new solutions to problems	Spreading an idea among individuals or organizations within a certain area or system (geographic, organisational, professional); ideas can be adapted to fit in different purposes or contexts	Communication Marketing Dissemination
Technology or skill		
Products, tools, techniques or practices	Increasing the number of people or places that use or apply a technology, practice or approach	Marketing Distribution Training Granting
Policy		
Codified statements that define plans or a course of action	Ensuring that ideas expressed as policy are transformed into behaviour throughout a place or jurisdiction (e.g. city, county, state, region, country)	Implementation

Source: Julia Coffman, 'Broadening the Perspective on Scale', *The Evaluation Exchange,* 15, no. 1 (Spring 2010): 3.

spreading ideas and gaining buy-in and adoption from other organizations and even entire populations.

The third framework, developed by Jeffrey Bradach and Abe Grindle of the Bridgespan Group and published in *Transformative Scale: The Future of Growing What Works,*[13] outlines two key lenses for scaling. The lens first examines organizational pathways, through which enterprises can build on or expand on their work. The second lens using a field-building pathway, considers opportunities to shape sectors and ecosystems and galvanize a range of actors to achieve a shared vision.

Interviews with social innovators and facilitators that support them reveal that many of these pathways are being utilized in the African context, with varying levels of success. Under the organizational pathways lens, a widely attempted approach at scaling on the African continent is **leveraging technology**. For example, Bridge International Academies operates a vertically integrated 'Academy-in-a-Box' model, and has re-engineered basic education, leveraging data,

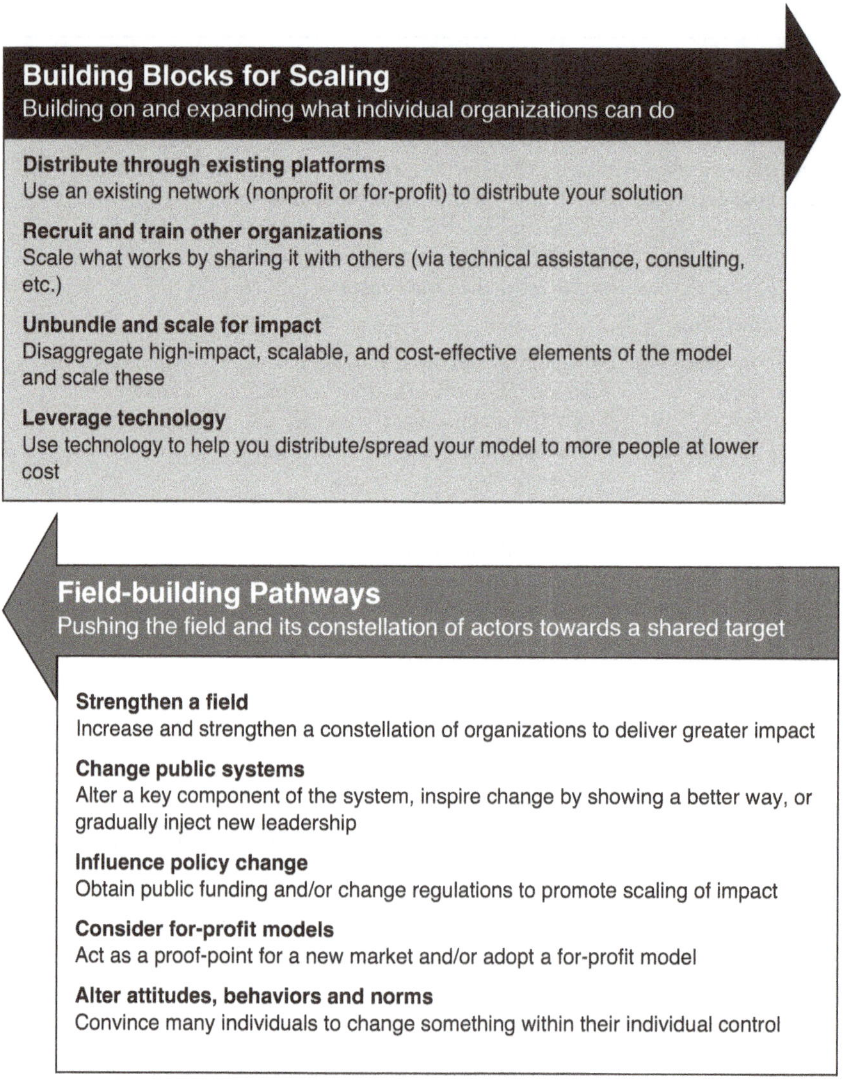

Building Blocks for Scaling
Building on and expanding what individual organizations can do

Distribute through existing platforms
Use an existing network (nonprofit or for-profit) to distribute your solution

Recruit and train other organizations
Scale what works by sharing it with others (via technical assistance, consulting, etc.)

Unbundle and scale for impact
Disaggregate high-impact, scalable, and cost-effective elements of the model and scale these

Leverage technology
Use technology to help you distribute/spread your model to more people at lower cost

Field-building Pathways
Pushing the field and its constellation of actors towards a shared target

Strengthen a field
Increase and strengthen a constellation of organizations to deliver greater impact

Change public systems
Alter a key component of the system, inspire change by showing a better way, or gradually inject new leadership

Influence policy change
Obtain public funding and/or change regulations to promote scaling of impact

Consider for-profit models
Act as a proof-point for a new market and/or adopt a for-profit model

Alter attitudes, behaviors and norms
Convince many individuals to change something within their individual control

Figure 1.2 Transformative scale pathways: The Bridgespan Group

Source: Bradach, J. and Grindle, A., *Transformative Scale: The Future of Growing What Works: Nine Strategies to Deliver Impact at a Scale that Truly Meets Needs.* The Bridgespan Group, February 2014.

and technology, to achieve scale. Bridge's operating model and reduced cost of service delivery enables it to cater for families who live on less than $2 a day, enabling them to enroll their children in the school. The first Bridge International Academy was established in 2009 in Kenya within Nairobi's Mukuru slum. In January 2015, Bridge had over a 100,000 students in 359 schools and opens a new academy every 2.5 days.

Another popular approach used by international organizations looking to scale their models to the African continent, is to **recruit and train champions to establish local entities.** Beyond providing technical assistance, knowledge sharing and supporting the emergence of strong governance structures, the initiatives drive themselves.

This approach has been utilized by Junior Achievement which has operations in 16 African countries and ENACTUS which works in nine. Similarly, since launching in 2007, Teach For All has grown to include 34 independent organizations, including its founding partners Teach For America and Teach First. They currently operate in every region of the world, including emerging entities in Nigeria, Ghana, Kenya, and South Africa. Teach For All forms partnerships with organizations that share the same theory of change and are committed to eight unifying principles, including placing teachers in schools for two years, measuring impact, partnering with public and private sectors, and remaining independent of government control.

Under the **field-building pathways** classification, there are also emerging examples of social innovations that are scaling by **changing public systems** and **influencing policy change.** Sadly, this is often one of the most difficult avenues for scaling, given the short-term focus of democracies in Sub-Saharan Africa and the doggedness required to sustain a campaign between subsequent administrations in order to change policy.

However, there are a few examples in the African context, specifically in the human rights and reproductive health space. Tostan,[14] established in Senegal in 1991, has used its human rights-based Community Empowerment Program (CEP) to engage over 7,000 communities from Djibouti, Guinea, Guinea-Bissau, Mali, Mauritania, Senegal, Somalia, and the Gambia. It provides communities with training and empowers them to draw their own conclusions about female genital cutting (FGC) and lead their own movements for change. As of March 2015, 86 communities have held public declaration ceremonies abolishing FGC.

Another example of field-building pathways is Action Health Incorporated (AHI)'s success at shaping policy and practice on sexuality education.[15] Based in Nigeria, AHI partnered with a range of local and international organizations and the government to scale up comprehensive sexuality education (CSE) using the Family Life and HIV Education (FLHE) curriculum. This curriculum provides a comprehensive approach to HIV prevention education and general sexual health at the secondary level of education. This innovation was rooted in the evidence that sexuality education reduces the risk of early and unprotected sex, unsafe abortion, transmission of HIV and other STDs, and maternal mortality.

Despite strong resistance to sexuality education, given the prevailing values and norms in religious circles in Nigeria, a concerted partnership between civil society, international development agencies, the government agencies, and funders, FLHE was eventually adopted at the federal and state levels.

Strengthening a field is another emerging pathway, largely being propelled by development partners and facilitators who are focused on priority sectors such as health, education, energy, agriculture, economic development and financial inclusion. For example, Enhancing Financial Innovation & Access (EFInA), which was created by the United Kingdom's Department for International Development (DFID), operates an innovation fund to encourage financial service providers to develop and launch products and services that would benefit the unbanked and under-banked low-income populations in Nigeria. It provides grant subsidies for commercial and policy-related initiatives, in order to mitigate financial risks that often hinder these innovations. To date, EFInA has supported financial services providers such as Paga, Guaranty Trust Bank, and Accion Microfinance Bank Limited to launch and scale products for the unbanked.

EFInA also collaborates with regulators, including the Central Bank of Nigeria, the National Pension Commission (PENCOM), and the Nigeria Deposit Insurance Corporation (NDIC), for the development and review of financial policies and regulations; including advocating for an agent banking regulation in 2013 to enable village shops to serve as agents for banks.

Since its creation in 2007 EFInA, working in partnership with a range of stakeholders, has transformed the financial services landscape from one that only banked 7 million customers in a country of 170 million, to one that currently banks over 30 million.

Finally, **adopting a for-profit model** is another pathway to scale. Farm Africa is a nonprofit that provides training and linkages to farmers in five countries in East Africa. It established Sidai Africa Ltd in 2011, a social enterprise – for-profit, which manages a network of franchised and branded Livestock Service Centres in Kenya. The Sidai centres are owned and run by qualified veterinarians, livestock technicians and professionals and provide animal health products and professional technical advice to farmers and pastoralists.

Ultimately, there are a wide range of approaches to scaling, as illustrated by the models and examples outlined above. Each organization, based on its vision, theory of change, mission, values and structure, determined which pathway was most suitable. Many of these examples will be explored in greater detail in subsequent chapters to highlight the strategic decisions they took around their business models, financing, and partnership strategies to ensure high-impact scaling.

Summary

This chapter introduces the critical building blocks for developing focused and strategic social innovations that can achieve large scale social impact. These include clearly outlining mission, values and vision statements and a theory of change, which enable the innovator to set clear objectives and boundaries. In addition, the innovator has to determine the most suitable structure for sustainable scaling – either nonprofit, for-profit or hybrid, based on the needs and income potential of the innovation. Finally, he or she has to identify appropriate pathways for scaling, selecting from a broad range of models – hinged on the nature of the innovation and the desired impact on society.

Notes

1   Mangan, Ben 2013. Stanford Social Innovation Review, 'The ugly truth about scale', March 4; www.ssireview.org/blog/entry/the_ugly_truth_about_scale
2   PATH 2015. 'Reimagining global health: 30 high-impact innovations to save lives', accessed 2015; www.path.org/features/innovations2015/#innovations
3   Ikamva Youth website, accessed July 10, 2015; http://ikamvayouth.org/about/mission-vision-values
4   One Acre Fund website, accessed August 10, 2015; www.oneacrefund.org/about-us/purpose-values/
5   One Acre Fund website, accessed November 10, 2015; www.oneacrefund.org/our-approach/vision
6   Kidogo website, accessed June 25, 2015; www.kidogo.co/our-philosophy/
7   Star, Kevin. Stanford Social Innovation Review, 'The eight word mission statement', accessed 2013; http://ssir.org/articles/entry/the_eight_word_mission_statement#sthash.v2bRTYbY.58LZv95t.dpuf
8   This registration is the most common type of legal status for a nonprofit organization registered in the United States exempt from federal income tax.
9   B Impact Assessment website, accessed on August 15, 2015; http://bimpact assessment.net/how-it-works/frequently-asked-questions/the-b-impact-score
10 B-Corp website, accessed July 14, 2015,/www.bcorporation.net/
11 Cooley, Larry and Kohl, Richard March 2006, Scaling Up: From Vision to Large-scale Change: A Management Framework for Practitioners, Management Systems International, Washington, DC.
12 Coffman, Julia 2010. 'Broadening the Perspective on Scale', The Evaluation Exchange.
13 Bradach, Jeffrey and Grindle, Abe: Transformative Scale: The Future of Growing What Works: Nine Strategies to Deliver Impact at a Scale that Truly Meets Needs, The Bridgespan Group, February 2014.
14 Tostan website, accessed March 2, 2015; www.tostan.org/female-genital-cutting
15 Silvia Huaynoca, Venkatraman Chandra-Mouli, NuhuYaqub Jr. and Donna Marie Denno (2014) 'Scaling up comprehensive sexuality education in Nigeria: from national policy to nationwide application, Sex Education, 14(2): 191–209; www.tand fonline.com/doi/pdf/10.1080/14681811.2013.856292

2 Sustainable business models that scale

Introduction

Following the development of clear visions, missions, values, and structures and the identification of the most appropriate pathways for scaling, the next step is the design of business models that are scalable. This often appears easy on paper, but is extremely difficult in practice. The average social innovator is motivated by a passion to solve a social problem and desires to produce the highest impact intervention to address that problem. This passion takes the social innovator down the path of designing a state-of-the-art intervention and pilot which often are not scalable.

Consider the Playpump example which effectively illustrates this phenomenon. In 2006, the Playpump was touted as one of the most innovative solutions to the challenge of water scarcity in villages across Africa. Harnessing the power of children at play, it was designed as a merry-go-round type device, installed and connected to a water pump. As children played on the merry-go-round, they would provide the energy for water to be pumped into a storage tank. The organization publicly shared its vision of building 4,000 Playpumps by 2010 to bring the 'benefit of clean drinking water to up to 10 million people'.

AOL's co-founder, Steve Case, and a range of other key leaders in the foundation sector were enthralled by the Playpump idea and provided support and funding for a scale-up. Sadly, the process of scaling up revealed a few fatal flaws:

- First, Playpumps cost four times the amount of a regular water pump.
- Second, when it broke, it was very difficult to repair.
- Third, an analysis by the *Guardian*,[1] revealed that kids would have to 'play' for 27 hours a day to meet the target of delivering water to 2,500 people per pump.

The reality is Playpumps only make sense under limited conditions such as when there is a large supply of high-quality groundwater, close to the surface, and when present infrastructure is insufficient.

The Playpump example illustrates the importance of designing and developing business models that scale, if possible, from the outset. However, for innovators who are stuck in the same predicament as the founders of the Playpump, it is never too late to reformulate and refine the innovation to ensure that it can scale.

Interviews with over 80 social innovators operating on the African continent reveal that the product or service innovations that have been able to scale have started with scaling as a goal from day one. To ensure sustainability, these initiatives are demand-driven – filling a significant gap in the lives of its target population. High-impact innovators have determined the cheapest way to deliver impact at scale and developed effective systems and structures to support their scaling effort. They have also leveraged technology, are highly dependent on a robust data tracking system to measure impact and engage local communities.

This chapter will address each of these components of business models that scale in detail – providing practical examples and key questions for social innovators to address.

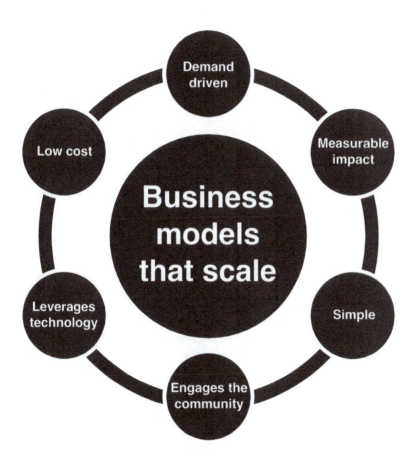

Figure 2.1 Components of business models that scale
Source: Developed by Ndidi Okonkwo Nwuneli.

Demand driven

The innovation landscape is replete with technology and process-driven inventions that were celebrated in industry circles, but never adopted and sustained by the target population. The sad reality is that most of these innovations were 'supply-driven', and not 'demand-driven', partly because those who design solutions are often far removed from the realities on the ground. They assume erroneously that the target population would be willing to utilize the intervention to improve their lives. However, there are countless examples of these types of interventions in a range of sectors, especially in the health and agriculture landscapes, that appear to work during the pilot phase – because they were fully funded or highly subsidized, but failed during the scale-up phase because they were not demand-driven.

The book *Growing Smartly: Scaling Seed Systems for Smallholder Farmers*, by the Syngenta Foundation for Sustainable Agriculture,[2] highlights the numerous innovations in improved seed varieties. Sadly, most remain in demonstration plots, but are never adopted by farmers, simply because the farmers struggle to see the need to substitute their current cultivation practices with new ones. According to the editor, Sara Boettiger, 'The farmer may need to learn the value of a new technology, but ultimately, if that technology does not hold sufficient value for a reasonable return on investment from the farmer's perspective, it will not be adopted.'

For true demand to be ascertained, it is imperative that the social innovator address key aspects of demand-awareness, availability, accessibility, affordability, and acceptability. For example, improved seeds which could triple the yields of maize farmers in Northern Ghana would only be used if they can find them easily in their local market or local agro-dealer shops, if they are affordable and if they look and feel like seeds – which is the acceptability component. However, proving that there is sustainable demand for the seeds requires that the farmers actually use the seeds, and are able to achieve considerably higher yields, which convinces them to buy the seeds over and over again.

It is important to recognize that innovators who have already gone down the path of pushing supply-driven strategies have to be willing to alter their approach or target customer base to achieve high-impact results. For example, Ashifi Gogo, a Ghanaian inventor, developed the concept of a Short Message Service (SMS)-based verification system, targeted at empowering customers shopping in the produce sections of grocery stores to verify the origin and organic history of their intended purchase. While exciting, no customer or key stakeholder was prepared to pay for the cost of the system. In a swift response, Dr. Gogo repositioned the same innovation to address a different problem – the billion dollar industry of counterfeit medicines – and the award-winning social enterprise Sproxil was born.

In 2009, Sproxil launched its Mobile Product Authentication™ (MPA™) technology in Nigeria to help patients avoid dangerous fake medicine at the point of sale. Using their mobile devices, the customer could verify the authenticity of any medicine with a single use code. This service generated significant demand from the government and regular citizens, who were concerned about the rising deaths over fake drugs, which according to the WHO[3] accounted for over 700,000 annual global deaths and 100,000 deaths in Africa, due to fake anti-malarial and tuberculosis drugs alone. In addition, there was significant demand from pharmaceutical companies and their distributors, given the rising loss of consumer confidence in recognized brands and the lost revenue in legal distribution channels due to the growth in the counterfeit industry.

Based on its early successes, Sproxil has established operations in the US, India, Pakistan, Ghana, Kenya and Nigeria, and even has a presence in Mexico.

The experience of Sproxil and other social innovations that have been able to scale on the African continent have demonstrated the importance of sustainable demand for a product or service in ensuring long term sustainability and impact.

BOX 2.1: KEY QUESTIONS FOR INNOVATORS

Is your business model demand-driven?

- Is this product or service needed? How do you know?
- Will enough people use it?
- Is any other group providing this intervention in your target community or region? (This will require a mapping of the market locally, nationally and globally – to determine whether an adapted franchise approach might be preferred.)
- For a product – is it acceptable, accessible, and affordable and is there considerable consumer awareness? If not, what would it take to educate consumers?
- If your innovation or entity that delivers it disappeared today, would anyone miss it?

Measurable impact

The days when a few good stories about the impact of interventions were enough to justify funding for scaling are long gone. All key stakeholders, especially funders and impact investors, are interested in understanding exactly how many people have been reached with the innovation and how it has changed their lives in a tangible and measureable way.

A highly publicized example of this phenomenon is the One Laptop Per Child (OLPC) initiative which was launched in 2006 by Professor Nicholas Negroponte of the Massachusetts Institute of Technology (MIT). OLPC[4] aims to provide:

each child with a rugged, low-cost, low-power, connected laptop, designed with hardware and software for collaborative, joyful, and self-empowered learning. With access to this type of tool, children are engaged in their own education, and learn, share, and create together. They become connected to each other, to the world and to a brighter future.

This initiative, implemented in over 15 countries in Africa, Asia and South America, has been highly criticized by evaluators and the media over findings released from the government of Peru which revealed that children who benefited from the low-cost laptops showed no improvement in test scores. These results generated significant backlash from the global media, including the *Economist*,[5] with headlines – 'Error message: A disappointing return from an investment in computing'. Skepticism about interventions that only measure the number of people reached or technological devices distributed, as opposed to impact, is understandable and can be avoided.

Contrast the experience of OLPC with the results of organizations such as One Acre Fund, which provides financing, training and access to inputs to over 300,000 smallholder staple-crop farmers operating in Burundi, Kenya, Rwanda and Tanzania. One Acre Fund has prioritized measuring its impact for four[6] key reasons:

- Prove: we have an obligation to farmers and to our donors to prove our impact. We also use impact data to make resource allocation decisions.
- Learn: we're constantly learning and evaluating so we can improve each individual programming unit.
- Improve: impact data helps us develop new life-improving products.
- Maintain: we use our impact data to maintain operational consistency across all geographies.

One Acre Fund measures its scale of impact. It also actively evaluates historical data and plans for future years – not just in terms of scale, but also impact.

In addition, One Acre Fund has an entire department called 'scale innovations' that focuses on improving the efficiency and effectiveness of the scaling effort, guided by a key formula: *Social Good = Reach × Impact*. Focused on achieving operational improvements, the team has focused on five key objectives:

1 Increase farmer-to-field officer ratio, a proxy for the cost-effectiveness of its model.
2 Increase 'site density,' i.e., the number of farmers in a given area who join One Acre Fund.
3 Streamline farmer repayment so that field staff can spend more time on what matters most.
4 Pilot credit scoring to target interventions for clients who will benefit most.
5 Increase client transaction size to generate more impact and higher margins with the same number of staff.

Table 2.1 One Acre Fund impact results

Year	2013 (actual)	2014 (actual)	2015 (end of year projected)	2016 (projected)
Scale				
Families served	130,400	203,600	305,000	420,000
Full-time staff	1,900	2,343	3,000	3,500
Impact				
$ Gain in farm income	$135*	$128	$135	$135
Gain in farm income	47%*	57%	50%	50%
Sustainability				
Loan repayment	99%	99%	97%+	97%+
Field sustainability	73%	74%	78%	82%

Source: One Acre Fund website, accessed June 7 2015, www.oneacrefund.org/results/impact/

Note: *2013 impact has been restated (from $139 to $135, and from 52 percent to 47 percent) to reflect some impact methodology changes in 2014 that we retroactively applied to 2013.

There are not many entities like One Acre Fund which actively prioritize measurement and evaluation, and use robust systems and structures for collecting high-quality data. In reality, most social innovators complain that the measurement and evaluation process is cumbersome and expensive. They also argue that the complexity of many social change interventions, the length of time required to achieve impact, and their need to collaborate with other organizations to achieve results, makes measuring impact extremely challenging. This is especially true in the health and education sectors.

The emerging focus on baselines and control groups and 'theory of change' models – where inputs, activities, outputs and outcomes are measured – are all useful tools that the sector is starting to leverage. However, this trend is being stifled by the nature of the data collection practices and the quality of the data produced by many government agencies in Africa which compels social innovators to engage in the expensive process of primary data collection.

In addition, scaling exacerbates the data collection challenge because it widens the distance between the social innovator and their customers. Quality control challenges worsen. It is much more difficult to maintain high standards across a large number of sites.

Regardless of these challenges, all innovators have to measure impact as a critical prerequisite for building credibility among customers and clients, raising financing for scaling from funders and investors, and forming strategic partnerships with the government and other key stakeholders.

The Evidence Continuum developed by Management Systems International (MSI)[7] outlines six key steps for demonstrating evidence, with minimal objective evidence and anecdotal reports at one end of the spectrum and evidence of impact and proven models on the other.

Indeed, every social entrepreneur aspires to move beyond nice stories to best practice and ultimately, policy change. This can only occur with strong evidence, rooted in credible measurement and evaluation.

Social innovators, who are committed to measuring their impact as they scale, have to take the six following critical steps.

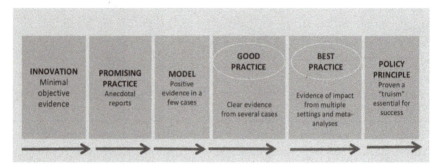

Figure 2.2 The evidence continuum

Source: Cooley, Larry and Lin, Johannes *Taking Innovations to Scale: Methods, Applications and Lessons,* Results for Development Institute, September 2014.

1   *Identify key indicators of impact for the direct and indirect customers or clients*

Every innovation team has to determine which indicators they will actively track in the short, medium and long term to gauge the impact of their interventions. For example, One Acre Fund not only tracks the number of farm families served, but also the percentage of loan repayment and the dollar increase in farm income, which is more indicative of impact. Similarly, Educate! which is focused on skills-based education to improve life outcomes for high school students, starting in Uganda, has developed a robust list of indicators that it tracks regularly and period-ically revises to maintain efficiency and serve program needs. A sample of indicators tracked by Educate! is outlined in Table 2.2.

There is no optimal number of indicators that organizations should track as long as they can manage their list effectively, the indicators are clear, and the method and frequency is well understood and followed by all the key stakeholders. Given the status of women on the African continent, it is also critical that all organi-zations actively include indicators that utilize a gender lens, measuring the impact of their interventions on women as beneficiaries.

2   *Conduct a baseline or identify a control group to demonstrate difference*

Results mean little unless they are compared against another standard – either those who have not benefited from the innovation – directly or indirectly, the norm, best case or even the worst case. Ideally, social innovators still in the start-up phase invest the time and energy to determine what the base case scenario is

Table 2.2 Sample of key indicators, methods and frequency utilized by Educate!

Indicator	Type	Method	Frequency
Percentage of Leadership & Entrepreneurship (LEC) lessons taught	Monitoring	SMS	Weekly
Scholar attendance at LEC lessons	Monitoring	SMS	Weekly
Scholar attrition at LEC lessons	Monitoring	SMS	Trimesterly
Number of scholars completing a leadership passbook or business skills portfolio	Monitoring	SMS	Bi-Annually
Percentage of YBE Meetings held	Monitoring	Smartphone	Bi-Weekly
Percentage of teachers attending Experience Association meetings	Monitoring	Smartphone	Monthly
Number of projects run by Student Business Clubs	Monitoring	Smartphone	Trimesterly
Cash profit of Student Business Clubs	Monitoring	Smartphone	Trimesterly
Head teacher rating of Educate! program	Monitoring	Paper-based	Trimesterly
Number of employees in each business	Evaluation	Paper-based	Before and after the program
Number of businesses started	Evaluation	Paper-based	
Employment rates (formal and informal)	Evaluation	Paper-based	
Savings behaviour & social protection	Evaluation	Paper-based	
Total earnings	Evaluation	Paper-based	
University enrollment	Evaluation	Paper-based	

before they introduce a pilot and then roll-out the innovation. Where credible government or development partner statistics are available, the organization may depend on this for one anchor. In addition, they should also conduct surveys to understand the depth of the needs – to enable effective targeting and prioritization.

For interventions, without an initial baseline, the innovators typically institute control groups. For example, in April 2015, Bridge International Academies organized common exams to be taken by 42 non-Bridge schools in Kenya. This provided the organization with a useful control group to measure the results of its own schools relative to others. Similarly, Ikamva Youth South Africa obtains regular data from the different municipalities of student outcomes of the general population and compares this to the results of its 'learners', who benefit from the tutoring and mentoring it provides.

3   Determine the most efficient and effective process for measuring impact at key milestones

The process of measuring impact – tracking the lives of the direct and indirect beneficiaries and comparing them with control groups is often cumbersome and expensive. As a result, organizations that scale at impact on the African continent demonstrate a commitment to developing efficient and effective processes for measuring impact. As indicated by the case of Educate! outlined above, some indicators such as attendance can be sent by field employees via a simple text message using a basic telephone, on a weekly basis. Other indicators such as skills gained or profits generated from student-run businesses require a more detailed assessment process, which is conducted less frequently, and sent from the field using a smartphone. Given the nature of interventions, some require a longer lead time to measure outcomes and incentives for individuals to respond to questions sent via telephone or email about their livelihoods and outcomes. Educate! monitors university enrollment and earnings after the participants have graduated from the program, via a paper-based evaluation. The Paradigm Initiative in Nigeria (PIN), which provides ICT and life skills to at-risk youth, withholds certificates until months after the program, when the participant is able to report on key impact indicators such as job placement and peer training. Other groups provide recharge cards and financial incentives to encourage program alumni to respond to periodic updates on their livelihoods and outcomes.

Technology and cross-sector partnerships are easing the cost and enhancing the efficiency of the measurement and evaluation process. Organizations, such as Dimagi, partner with civil society, development partners, and government agencies across Africa to support their data and impact assessment processes.

4   *Periodically engage independent audits or verification*

Global best practice stipulates the need for independent consultants or agencies to conduct audits of the innovation on a periodic basis to verify the in-house results. These independent audits and assessments are extremely useful for the organization, enabling it to gain new insights and feedback for enhancing the impact of the innovation. In addition, it enhances the credibility of the results of the organization and invariably enables it to gain support from a range of partners.

Independent assessments are often too expensive for small organizations to undertake. However, there is a growing number of funders who are willing to cover the cost of independent audits to verify the impact of an innovation, especially one that they are funding. These audits enable them to determine if they should continue funding the work and where the key levers exist for accelerating impact. In addition, independent assessments demand some level of engagement from the senior management team of the organizations for the kick-off and wrap-up phases.

5   *Refine or change approach based on results*

Data generated from internal and independent measurement and evaluation activities and audits are periodically reviewed by the management team and the board, to provide significant insights into the impact of the innovations. These insights enable the team to refine their current approach or change course based on poor or positive results. It is important to recognize that failures are also extremely useful learning experiences which inform capital and human resource allocation decisions and also influence future funder engagement. Depending on the nature of the data collection and synthesis process, further analysis might be required on grey areas prior to taking decisive action.

6   *Develop and implement a robust communication strategy to share results broadly with critical stakeholders*

Once impact is measured, the results – whether positive or negative – should be shared with the key stakeholders involved in the scale-up effort to inform their strategic planning process and to enable them to make key decisions regarding resource allocations. Depending on the innovation, results could also be shared through the mass and social media and public forums, conferences and round-tables to raise awareness, change mindsets and shape policy. For example, organizations such as One Acre Fund and LEAP Africa publish their results on their website and in their annual reports. In addition, opportunities for improvement and lessons learned should be shared with key stakeholders to advance the field and inform specific changes in the ecosystem.

BOX 2.2: KEY QUESTIONS FOR INNOVATORS

Is your innovation achieving measureable impact?

- In the pilot phase of the innovation, what impact did the initiative achieve? Why? How did you measure this impact? Can others take credit for the same impact?
- What key indicators do you currently measure? How are they measured? What is the frequency and mode of data collection?
- What baseline or control group do you utilize to demonstrate a comparison between your intervention and the status quo? Is this credible? What does it demonstrate?
- How has measurement and evaluation of the impact of your innovation informed your approach, changed your strategy or influenced behavior of key stakeholders?
- Has the intervention been tested for a long enough period to prove that it actually meets a need relative to alternatives? Is this need sustainable?
- What opportunities for improvement or failures have you identified and how have they shaped your activities or informed your decision making process?
- Have you utilized external evaluators to test and verify the impact of your interventions? What did this process reveal?
- How do you communicate your impact to internal and external stakeholders?

Ultimately, social innovations need a robust measurement and evaluation system complete with clear indicators, mechanisms for data collection and synthesis, comparisons with base lines and control groups, periodic external audits, and effective communication of results. It is these organizations that will be able to sustain long-term impact and generate support from a broad range of stakeholders.

Simplicity and Replicability

Complex interventions are difficult to scale. Innovators must divide complex solutions into relatively simple components, codify them in manuals, standardize the intervention process using technology, and remove any ambiguity or room for human interpretation and potential for error.

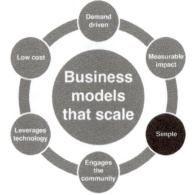

BOX 2.3: KEY QUESTIONS FOR INNOVATORS

Is your model simple enough?

- Can you explain your model in 30 seconds? Is your 'elevator pitch' clear and compelling?
- What key systems, structures, operating strategy and technologies were critical to the early successes?
- What aspect of the systems, structures and operating strategy will need to be altered or modified to enable the scaling process?
- How can technology be leveraged to simplify and standardize the business model?

Consider LEAP Africa's experience with scaling, when it transitioned from its Youth Leadership Program, where it provided direct leadership training to hundreds of youth between the ages of 18 and 30, to its Leadership, Ethics and Civics (LEC) program, where it provides training for teachers who then deliver its curriculum to thousands of students. In order to effectively scale without sacrificing the quality of the experience, the team invested in simplifying the methodology and instituting systems and structures to ensure standardization. It codified the teaching methodology, developed a trainer's manual and a student manual, complete with interactive exercises and games, and a feedback mechanism for both the students and the teachers. In addition, the organization matched volunteers to each school to actively track the execution and impact of the youth Change projects. More recently, LEAP has invested in elearning tools, starting with E-integrity to standardize the training methodology on ethics and ensure a consistent message and training experience.

The process of simplifying business models is extremely difficult, especially in specific sectors, such as healthcare, where there are often multi-pronged interventions to address the challenges that confront the masses of people. However, regardless of the industry, social innovators have to take a few decisive steps:

- **Prioritize:** this essentially entails laying out all the steps and processes required for the innovation and determining what is most important for impact. Engaging a few external stakeholders with fresh eyes also enables the innovator to see the solutions from a new lens.
- **Leverage technology:** there are many aspects of service delivery models that can be rapidly simplified by leveraging technology, especially for training, program delivery, data entry, and analysis. This also reduces the costs and improves the efficiency and effectiveness of the operations.
- **Leverage partnerships:** where possible, social innovators who are committed to scaling streamline their activities and partner with others to manage non-core activities. They also leverage the infrastructure, logistical support and assistance that other organizations are able to offer, assuming the partnerships are mutually beneficial, based on shared values, mutual respect and trust.
- **Codify:** too often social innovators do not invest the time and energy required to develop systems and structures for standardizing operations and product and service delivery. This limits scaling, especially as the innovation spreads across geographies. Social innovators who scale models across communities and whose frameworks are widely adopted develop operating manuals, check lists, reporting mechanisms, and effective systems and structures to enable them deliver standardized programs and services.

Simplifying procedures, processes and instituting systems and structures are critical to effective business models that scale. This allows for standardization, consistency across geographies and sectors, and ensures that the impact of the innovation is not compromised with scaling.

Cost of impact

As illustrated in the case of the Playpump discussed earlier, innovations that are scalable have to be low-cost; otherwise they are prohibitive relative to alternatives and costly to implement and sustain.

What are unit economics?

Rooted in business, unit economics is essentially the cost of delivering one product or service to a customer. In the social sector, with a focus on impact, the meaning of the word is extended beyond product or service delivery to impact – a change in the life of the beneficiary because of that product or service. This is often difficult to determine, especially if that change process extends over a period of time.

Interventions that are scalable have to develop low-cost products, services and support structures, which are efficient and effective, without diminishing their impact.

For example, Jacaranda, a social enterprise based in Kenya, is transforming the maternal care landscape in the region through its concerted effort to provide low-cost and high quality care to pregnant women, directly reducing the high rates of maternal mortality.

Jacaranda is able to deliver a baby at only $80 for a normal delivery, 30–70 percent of the price of similar services at other facilities. It also charges $5 for an initial antenatal care visit and about $1 for each proceeding family planning visit. This incredible cost structure has been achieved by training healthcare workers, utilizing technology for scheduling and record keeping and implementing checklists and algorithms to standardize care.

Jacaranda was accredited by the Kenyan National Health Insurance Fund (NHIF) in mid-2014, and is gradually scaling by transferring its best practice approaches in maternal health to the broader public sector healthcare landscape.

Similarly, the Paradigm Initiative in Nigeria (PIN), a social enterprise based in Nigeria which provides ICT and life skills training to unemployed youth, was able to reduce its unit cost of service delivery and impact from $1,000 to $100 per participant. This dramatic reduction was achieved by more effective asset utilization – shifting from renting spaces for training sessions to long-term leases and engaging in training two batches of students per day, ensuring that it is operating at full capacity. This approach enabled PIN to scale to four locations across Nigeria.

In addition, PIN youth have to wait for seven to eleven months to get their certificates. In this timeframe, they are required to send monthly reports (a minimum of six reports) and provide 10 percent of their income to the program to enable another young person from their community to receive the same training. This process does not only allow PIN to generate earned income, but also minimizes the staff cost devoted to follow-up and tracking of its beneficiaries.

Finally, consider the unit cost pricing methodology used by Riders for Health, an international, not-for-profit social enterprise which works across Africa. Riders provides transportation and logistics services typically for ministries of health, enabling them to reach the rural and underserved communities. It manages and maintains fleets of vehicles for governments and has developed an innovative unit cost mechanism for its transport asset management program, called Cost-Per-Kilometer (cpk).[8] This is calculated by dividing the *Total cost of fleet management* by *Total distance traveled* (km).

The total cost includes both fixed and variable costs and encompasses fuel, replacement parts, technical and management staff, infrastructure and ongoing maintenance costs, over the lifetime of the vehicles. The distance figure per motorcycle/vehicle is taken by technicians who read each vehicle's odometer regularly and calculate vehicle mileage since the last reading.

- Fixed costs are proportional to the fleet size and dispersion. Infrastructure requirement is a key determinant of fixed costs and financing cost – fixed monthly, depending on the terms of loan repayment.
- Variable costs include fuel and replacement parts – a function of distance covered by fleet and technical staff which is a function of fleet size. This also includes the accumulation of capital needed for the replacement motorcycles and vehicles.

This model keeps Riders for Health focused on payment for performance, enables reliable budgeting and increases the controls for effective vehicle usage. It essentially keeps Riders focused on delivering value to its customers, and ensures that it only receives payments if the vehicles run and if Riders delivers on its mandate.

BOX 2.4: KEY QUESTIONS FOR INNOVATORS

How much does it cost to make an impact on a life?

- What is the cost of providing this innovation to achieve the desired impact for one client/beneficiary?
  - What are the fixed costs?
  - What are the variable costs?
  - What are the hidden costs (includes in-kind, time devoted by volunteers, discounts on items etc.)?
- Can this target customer or client pay for the service?
- Are there enough people who match his or her profile who can cover their own costs?
- Is there a sustainable financial model for this intervention or will it have to be subsidized in perpetuity?

The issues of financial management and costing are explored in greater detail in Chapter 4, 'Financing scaling'.

Ultimately, low-cost business models scale because limited funds can be spread to generate more impact, and are typically more economical and self-sustaining, because they are more affordable, especially for lower income populations.

Technology for scaling

Interviews with a broad range of social innovators in the public, private and nonprofit sectors emphasize the growing role of technology in driving social innovation. Technology supports product or service delivery, simplifies and standardizes business processes, and measurement and evaluation, accelerates communications with all stakeholders, and reduces costs.

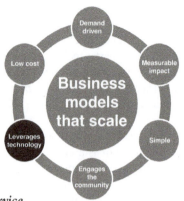

Utilizing technology to facilitate product/service delivery

Consider the Growth Enhancement Scheme (GES) launched by Dr. Akinwumi Adesina, the former Minister of Agriculture of the Federal Republic of Nigeria. This public sector intervention, which utilized the Electronic Wallet System, attempted to block the massive corruption in the distribution of seeds and fertilizers to smallholder farmers.

Introduced in 2012 as part of the Agricultural Transformation Agenda, the Electronic Wallet System enables smallholder farmers to obtain subsidized electronic vouchers for seeds and fertilizers directly on their mobile phones. These vouchers ensure that the farmers benefit from inputs (seeds at no cost and 50 percent subsidy on fertilizers) from private sector agricultural input dealers.

In two years GES had reached millions of farmers and has transformed the private sector inputs market, spurring the emergence of 80 seed companies when four major companies dominated the sector prior to GES. It has also led to the emergence of hundreds of agrodealers, private companies that sell inputs to farmers, across Nigeria.

Utilizing technology to facilitate payment

M-KOPA provides off-grid energy solutions with operations across East Africa. All revenues are collected in real-time via mobile money systems. An embedded GSM sensor in each solar system allows M-KOPA to monitor real-time performance and regulate usage based upon payments. This connected system allows M-KOPA to process over 10,000 mobile payments per day via the company's proprietary cloud platform, M-KOPAnet.

Utilizing technology to enhance and reduce the costs of communication

Slum2School, an organization driven by young volunteers, works in slums across Lagos, actively utilizing technology. According to Otto Orondaam, the founder, 80 percent of Slum2School's meetings are organized either through Google hangouts or Skype calls. This connects the volunteers who are abroad and also reduces the cost of physical meetings. Otto notes, 'Every team and department has a closed circuit chat group, either on WhatsApp or Blackberry messenger, and this connects everyone 24/7.'

Utilizing technology to standardize support and monitor impact

Dimagi, which works across Africa in partnership with funders, international NGOs and governments, offers an open source mobile platform which supports frontline workers to deliver services and monitor impact. Over the past decade, Dimagi has supported a range of initiatives in the health, agriculture, and education sectors, including active roles in the fight against the Ebola crises in Guinea and Liberia. In Burkina Faso, it partnered with Terre Des Hommes (TdH), the London School of Hygiene and Tropical Medicine (LSHTM), and the University Research Company (URC) to introduce the Integrated e-Diagnostic Approach (IeDA). The goal of IeDA was to directly reduce infant mortality by training nurses to better manage the quality of healthcare services via a diagnostic support tool, enabling nurses to follow healthcare protocols and actively monitor impact, using a tablet-based mobile application and web dashboard. The system also automatically backed up and stored patient data, and enabled project and Ministry staff to view reports in real time. This intervention was implemented in over 100 clinics across Burkina Faso and significantly transformed the lives of 175,000 children.

Technology for improved effectiveness

As noted in Chapter 1, Bridge International Academies utilizes technology for all aspects of its operations. First, Bridge International Academies engages research associates who utilize a digital survey platform to determine the potential catchment area for the school and total population available. It conducts in-depth, in-home interviews of at least 50 households in each community to fully understand family preferences and needs. It also uses geo-tagging to calculate how far children have to walk and performs catchment analysis, which in turn drives decisions around real estate acquisition. In addition, using the Academy Manager's smartphone, teachers download weekly guidelines, enabling the organization to enhance its teaching methodology and content in real time. In addition, teachers are required to sync their tablets with the Academy Manager's smartphone each morning, which allows headquarters to track teacher tardiness and absenteeism. Any absence of a teacher triggers a message to the teacher's tablet and a substitute teacher is automatically called to the site. Finally, all fees and costs are paid through mobile payment systems, which can be tracked on that smartphone and by headquarters.

These examples represent a fraction of the examples of social innovators who are utilizing a range of free and low-cost technology tools to not only ease the cost of product or program delivery, but also enhance the impact of their intervention, enabling them to communicate more effectively, measure impact, track costs and publicize results.

BOX 2.5: KEY QUESTIONS FOR INNOVATORS

How do you currently leverage technology?

Do you use technology to:

- Ease communications:
  - within your team?
  - between your organization and its beneficiaries/clients/customers?
  - with other stakeholders?
- Measure impact; if so how?
- Simplify and standardize operations, such as:
  - training?
  - payment collection?
- Improve your effectiveness?

What other areas of your operations or business model would benefit from the use of technology?

Engaging the community

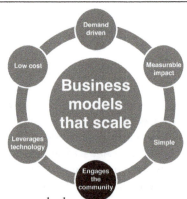

Most social innovations cannot scale sustainably if they do not have some local buy-in and support. As reinforced by the example of Tostan, described in Chapter 1, engagement with communities enables the scaling of ideologies and the change of long-held cultural beliefs which have historically had a negative impact on society.

Indeed, innovations that are scaling have worked diligently to invest early on to cultivate some champions in the community and maintain regular communications with them. In order to achieve this, they often actively map key stakeholders, understand the key actors and how to interface with them and form strategic partnerships. They also actively recruit employees from the community and serve beneficiaries in the community. Finally, they ensure ethnic, religious and gender diversity in the leadership and boards of the innovations.

For example, the successful scaling of MPedigree, established by Ghanaian entrepreneur, Bright Simmons, who first commenced operations in Ghana and then expanded to Nigeria, Kenya and eventually India, has been hinged on its community engagement. According to him, 'our systems, from cutting-edge technology to innovative partnerships, ensure that such critical products reach consumers in the right condition, protected from counterfeiting, diversion, tampering, and other supply chain abuses'. In Ghana, MPedigree not only engages with the local and national governments, local pharmaceutical firms such as LaGray, Dannex, Tobinco, Danadams, Kama and Starwin, but also partnered with the Pharmaceutical Society of Ghana to launch www.preventfaking.com. This engagement has enabled the company to build broad-based awareness among pharmacists and employees of pharmaceutical companies, ensuring that they not only protect the industry from fake drugs through their own activities, but also serve as champions for consumer awareness and behavior changes.

Similarly, Bridge International Academies, from the stage of deciding whether to open a school in a community, the team meets with local leaders to introduce the organization and assess that community's need and appetite for low-cost private schooling options. These community leaders become a strong resource providing referrals for community residents who eventually become engaged as teachers and Academy Managers.

Bridge also works closely with neighboring schools and national school organizations, in order to drive learning gains and to build a coalition of education providers for low-income populations.

BOX 2.6: KEY QUESTIONS FOR INNOVATORS

How engaged are you with your community?

- Do you have champions in your community?
- Do you hire or engage volunteers from your community?
- What strategies do you utilize to build broad-based awareness and support from your community to support your business model?
- What steps can you take to increase your community engagement to enable the scaling of your business model?

Strategies for community engagement will be explored in greater detail in Chapter 5, 'Partnerships for scaling'.

Summary

Business models that scale in the African context have to be demand-driven, high impact and simple, low cost, leverage technology and engage the community. It is important to recognize that the process of developing a suitable business model for scaling takes time and is iterative, with constant learning, change and refinement. In addition, it also requires that innovators invest in measurement and evaluation and knowledge management systems, financial management systems and the codification of their operating models to ensure consistency throughout the scaling process.

Notes

1   Chambers, Andrew, 'Africa's not-so-magic roundabout', *Guardian* November 24, 2009; www.theguardian.com/commentisfree/2009/nov/24/africa-charity-water-pumps-roundabouts

2   Boettiger, Sara 2014 *Growing Smartly: Scaling Seed Systems for Smallholder Farmers,* Syngenta Foundation for Sustainable Agriculture.

3   Sambira, Jocelyne May 2013 *Counterfeit Drugs Raise Africa's Temperature: Africa Renewal*, page 5. See more at: www.un.org/africarenewal/magazine/may-2013/counterfeit-drugs-raise-africa%E2%80%99s-temperature#sthash.O1RMeOg6.dpuf

4   One Laptop per Child website, accessed July 1, 2015; http://one.laptop.org/about/mission

5   'Error message: A disappointing return from an investment in computing', *The Economist*, April 7, 2012; www.economist.com/node/21552202

6   One Acre Fund website, accessed on June 7, 2015; www.oneacrefund.org/results/methodology

7   Cooley, Larry and Lin, Johannes 2014 *Taking Innovations to Scale: Methods, Applications and Lessons*, Results for Development Institute, September 2014.

8   Riders for Health 2013 *Riders' PPP model: innovation in pricing and capital finance*, 5th International Social Innovation Research Conference, ISIRC, Saïd Business School, University of Oxford. September 2013.

3   Talent for scaling

Introduction

When asked about the biggest challenge to scaling on the African continent, over 60 percent of the social innovators cite human capital. They complain about the challenges associated with attracting and retaining skilled, passionate and committed employees, who will not only embrace their vision, but also own and amplify it.

This talent challenge is a serious constraint to growth in all sectors of the economy on the African continent. Weak education and years of underinvestment by many African governments have produced a generation of unskilled and under-skilled workers. In addition, international opportunities abound for the most highly motivated and skilled – resulting in thousands of African doctors, nurses and academics moving to or remaining in Europe and the United States, instead of in their home countries.

However, social entrepreneurs face an even greater challenge because their salaries are uncompetitive relative to those offered by large corporate organizations. Unlike the public or international development sectors that offer job security, perks and a defined work schedule, social innovators expect their team members to work overtime, with limited perks and job security and to solve difficult social problems, often in challenging environments. This leads to a high rate of burn out and rampant poaching by development agencies, who can easily attract star employees who crave a better lifestyle and job security.

In spite of the hurdles that social innovators typically have to face, there are a few social innovators on the African continent that have been able to attract, engage, train, and retain talent for scaling. This chapter provides insights into their experiences and critical lessons for those who are still struggling to emulate them.

This chapter focuses narrowly on the experiences of innovators who have established nonprofits, social enterprises or social ventures. It is divided into four sections – Building a strong talent base, Structuring human resources for scale, Building and sustaining a culture of innovation and Restructuring your team for scaling. It is also important to note that many of the strategies shared in this chapter are applicable in any context, as they are typically recognized as best practice strategies for attracting, training and retaining talent for scaling.

Building a strong talent base

The social innovator has a critical role to play as the leader of the innovation. He or she is responsible for setting and communicating the vision, galvanizing others to buy into the vision, and infusing all key stakeholders with passion and a culture of teamwork, trust and impact.

However, the founder or initiator of a social innovator cannot achieve widespread impact at scale, working in isolation. Every social innovation needs to build a committed board of directors, engage partners and capable and committed team members. They also have to develop and implement strategies for attracting and recruiting, screening, motivating and retaining talent.

Building a committed board of directors

Instituting a board of directors from inception always differentiates a one-person-organization from an enduring enterprise. A strong board has oversight and fiduciary responsibility by law; however specifics of the roles and responsibilities of boards vary across Africa based on national laws.

Best practice[1] boards enhance the organization's credibility, provide advice and support, assist with fundraising efforts, evaluate the activities of the CEO/ executive director and challenge the organization to aim high and achieve results. This group typically consists of legal, finance and accounting, branding and communications and subject matter experts, who understand the industry and can complement the innovator's skills and experiences. Ideal boards have between five and nine members who commit to actively participating in at least four board meetings a year (this may vary depending on the organization's lifecycle and its needs) and committee meetings, as required.

Boards within organizations that scale impact are diverse, representing the gender, geographic, religious and ethnic and demographics groups in the region in which the social initiative operates.

Board members of nonprofits typically do not receive compensation for their services on the board; in fact, they are expected to provide financial and in-kind support to the organization. In return, they are made to feel valued and actively engaged in the organization's activities in order to gain a deeper appreciation for its work and impact. Social ventures and for-profits often offer sitting fees and other perks when they are able to achieve sustainable growth and profitability.

It is also important that board members have clear term limits, to allow for the infusion of 'new blood' and energy. Ideally, they serve for three-year terms, renewable for a second term, if appropriate. In addition, the boards have annual evaluations to measure their effectiveness and the contribution of individual members.

BOX 3.1: KEY QUESTIONS FOR INNOVATORS

How effective is your board?

- Do you have the most suitable board members for your organization? Do they have the right set of skills, experiences and values? Do they have passion and commitment? Are they willing to invest the time and energy required to enable the organization to scale?
- If you do not have the most suitable board members, could you consider others in your various networks: personal, professional, extracurricular, investors or even members of the senior management of your organization? (Each candidate must be subjected to a thorough screening process and must be selected based on their capacity to contribute to the board and the organization.)
- How frequently does your board meet?
- Does your board have an annual evaluation process to measure its own performance?
- Does it evaluate the organization at least once semi-annually?
- Does it formally assess the performance of the CEO/ED at least once a year?
- What specific steps should you take to enhance the effectiveness of your board?

For example, LEAP Africa constituted a strong board from inception. As the founder, I resisted the temptation to populate the board with friends or family members. I actively identified individuals that I respected, and who shared my passion for leadership development in Africa, especially among youth and entrepreneurs. They also shared my values of integrity and hard work and commitment, by devoting their time, resources and intellect to pushing the organization to achieve results. Our pioneer board consisted of the following individuals, who brought key skills to the organization:

- Mr. Olusegun Olujobi: Accenture partner, strategic thinker and problem solver with broad-based private sector experience.
- Mrs Maryam Uwais: respected lawyer with vast networks around Nigeria and a heart for development, especially among women.
- Mrs Nadu Denloye: respected entrepreneur in the information, communication and technology sector with a strong passion for youth development, training, coaching and mentoring.
- Mr. Folu Ayeni: respected entrepreneur with strong marketing and sales experience.
- Mr. Fabian Ajogwu: respected lawyer and professor at the Lagos Business School, with extensive experience supporting entrepreneurs.

This board represented the gender and ethnic diversity of Nigeria, but more importantly, was composed of passionate people, who leveraged their experiences, skills and networks to propel the organization. Through their engagement on the board, they gained a deep respect for each other and became lifelong friends and supporters of LEAP Africa.

Engaging partners

A growing number of social innovations that are scaling on the African continent are run by two to three partners who share a passion, values and complementary skills and have decided to work together to achieve impact. Notably difficult, the key to successful partnerships has been the founders' willingness to split roles from the onset and to stick to their core strengths. According to Ayodeji Adewunmi, co-founder of Jobberman, an online job portal that has transformed Nigeria's employment landscape, in an interview for this book – 'having co-Founders with complementary skills is not only desirable but important.' Ayodeji and two of his close friends, Opeyemi Awoyemi and Olalekan Olude from the Obafemi Awolowo University (OAU), decided to partner to create jobs for themselves and millions of other unemployed youth. Similarly, Bosun Tijani, Tunji Eleso and Femi Longe, who met through AIESEC[2] club during their days as students in different universities, built strong bonds by working on smaller initiatives together before establishing the widely successful Co-Creation Hub in Lagos. According to Femi, the values and respect they share has been critical to their successful partnership.

Beyond establishing formal business partnerships from the onset, social innovators should actively leverage local and international partnerships to deepen their skills, capacity and efficiency, and to extend their reach and support network. Jobberman has also actively leveraged partnerships. Ayodeji asserts,

> We are fortunate to have also partnered with two of the most iconic names in the world of online recruitment globally, SEEK, the most profitable job site in the world, and Tiger Global, the largest investor in online recruitment in the world.

The partnership and board experiences of social innovators on the African continent reveal seven key criteria for selecting board members and partners, similar to experiences shared by other entrepreneurs across the globe. Select individuals who:

- share your values of hard work, integrity and accountability;
- share your vision and passion to address the social problem;
- compliment your skills and experience and fill specific skill gaps;
- have a track record of success and credibility;
- are willing to take on and share responsibilities;
- you respect.

Engaging a capable and committed management team and staff

Every innovator committed to scaling has a strong management cadre, composed of a strong Chief Financial Officer (CFO) and Chief Operating Officer (COO). Different terms are used to describe these roles, depending on the size of the company and the nature of its operations. However, it is critical that at least one of the job descriptions focuses on the accounting and financial management of the company, and another on ensuring operating efficiency and effectiveness.

Beyond key technical skills, the management team has individuals who oversee communications or external relations and measurement and evaluation. These individuals possess the right balance of business acumen, knowledge, strong technical, communication and interpersonal skills. Their values also mirror the values of the organization – rooted in a strong work ethic, and integrity.

In addition to the management team, social innovations that scale have a significant number of people to execute the projects. As a result, the social innovator and management team often make a concerted effort to find strong candidates within the communities in which they work. They actively determine whether they need full-time or contract staff for the available positions, or if they can leverage volunteers, short-term consultants, or fellows to meet their specific organizational needs.

Volunteers

Social innovations operating in Africa, like many of their counterparts in other parts of the globe, leverage volunteers for short- and long-term interventions. Some organizations even encourage individuals to volunteer as a pathway to paid employment. Others recognize this group as a pool of talent for training, facilitation, and support for key events or activities. For example, both LEAP Africa and the FATE Foundation in Nigeria maintain a list of over 1,000 volunteers who support training programmes for youth and entrepreneurs. These volunteers typically have full-time jobs, but are committed to giving back to their communities, and are willing to devote two to three hours per week to supporting formal programmes.

Fellows

Some social innovators attract local and international fellows for short periods to work on a specific task. Fellows are recruited from leading business schools or consulting firms. A few impact investors' innovations such as Acumen and LGT Venture Philanthropy operate fellows programs. These programs attract mission-driven high achievers from across the globe who commit to spending nine to 12 months within an investee company, supporting a key aspect of their operations. The Acumen East Africa Fellows Program, a one-year, fully-funded leadership program, enrolls 20 fellows from across East Africa annually. The fellows are provided with five week-long seminars focused on building their financial and operational skills, and connecting them to the local and global community. International fellows often benefit from free housing, transportation and a stipend. This cost is typically borne by the social innovator or the impact investor or shared by both, and is often prohibitive for smaller, local organizations.

Short-term consultants

When social enterprises or nonprofits require targeted expertise and interventions in key areas of work, they also engage short-term consultants. Global best practice stipulates that social innovators engage in a formal Request for Proposal (RFP) process to identify the most suitable consultant. Given the significant variability of skills and capabilities of short-term consultants, social innovators always assess a minimum of three proposals to gauge the suitability of the proposed approach, the proposed budget and work plan. They also check references to ensure that they engage individuals who have a positive track-record and significant expertise. Formal contracts are critical to ensure that both the consultants' and the organization's expectations are aligned, with clear timelines for deliverables and payments linked to clear milestones.

It is important to recognize that sometimes volunteers, fellows, and consultants may prove to be more expensive than full-time hires, especially if they are recruited from a different city and require housing and transportation. These costs, in many African cities, prove prohibitive and sometimes detract from the cost savings that organizations expect to generate from engaging them in the first place.

Outsourcing

It is imperative for founders and management teams of social innovations to recognize that some aspects of their operations can be outsourced to other entities which are better positioned to manage them. The aspects of an operation that should be outsourced should be determined by the type of products, services, or processes that the organization engages in. For example, while some organizations outsource measurement and evaluation functions to information, communication and technology companies, others in the health sector such as Jacaranda outsource their need for ambulance services to bring their high risk patients to private clinics in Kenya.

Social innovators always need to weigh their organizational needs against their budgets to determine whether to hire full-time employees, engage volunteers, fellows or short-term consultants or even outsource specific functions. Ultimately, their goal is to minimize their overhead costs while leveraging talent and expertise in the community or from across the globe to drive high-impact scaling.

Attracting and recruiting talent

> Founders typically have the passion and skills to start, but finding talent to fill the 2 to 20 person slots in a growing company is really difficult – finding great joiners is one of the biggest challenges facing founders.
>
> (Ross Baird of Village Capital)

The quote by Ross Baird, an impact investor who has supported over 20 social innovators on the African continent, is echoed by others in the sector. Clearly, the recruitment process is a critical phase in building a dream team that can lead the scaling effort. The strategies that are utilized for finding talent vary, based on the positions, the nature of engagement, the level of skill and responsibility required, and compensation. It is important that social innovators create organizational charts and develop clear job descriptions, and review and refine them at least once a year. These charts will inform the hiring process, ensure organizational alignment, and enhance the efficiency and effectiveness of the recruiting process.

The innovators who have been able to attract talent have utilized a range of strategies, including enhancing their image, leveraging stakeholder networks, using technology and recruitment agencies, and engaging the community.

Enhance image

Social innovators, who are able to attract mission-driven high achievers, actively develop and promote a positive reputation. This includes being recognized as high-impact, cutting-edge, and innovative. This reputation is actively promoted through social and traditional media and ultimately generates unsolicited interest from strong performers, who are drawn to a culture and reputation, and have a desire to have meaningful impact in society. According to the founders of Sanergy in Kenya, their best employees came to them from well-established multinational and international development organizations, after reading about their innovative model in the press, driven by a desire to make a difference and transform lives.

In order to sustain any positive image in the public domain, there has to be significant substance. As a result, it is imperative that social innovators work diligently to create transparent and accountable organizations that have a strong reputation for ethics and impact. This essentially means that the entity responsible for scaling an innovation actively engages in and publishes its annual financial audits and impact results. It also empowers its team members and builds ownership and strong relationships with key stakeholders in the public, private and non-profit sectors.

Leverage strong stakeholder networks

Referrals are often cited as one of the most important avenues for attracting talent. As a result, social innovators typically leverage their boards, staff, partners and beneficiaries to serve as human resource ambassadors and recruiters and encourage them to circulate clear job descriptions and generate significant interest in the organization. Some social innovators even offer financial incentives to employees to refer capable individuals who eventually get hired. Some innovators also leverage networks to African Diaspora populations in the United States and the United Kingdom, and links to universities that have career fairs for prospective employers during their Africa related conferences. One of the most notable employment fairs is held annually at the Harvard Business School Africa Business Conference which attracts over 1,200 participants.

Leverage digital media

Many social innovators are increasingly leveraging online media through their organization or partner and network websites and free or low-cost online search firms to find suitable team members. According to Otto Orondaam, the founder of Slum2School which operates schools in urban slums in Nigeria, interviewed for this book,

> Our major source of talent and human resource is through our volunteer engagement model. Since inception in 2012, we have worked with over 5,000 volunteers on various short and long term projects. We have channels for volunteer recruitment, mainly online, through our website and advertisement on different blog platforms.

Online job listings on recruitment websites are often reposted by other sites, and this leads to a deluge of applications which the management team has to sift through. While often a cumbersome process, some social innovators prefer this approach because it is low cost and has a wide reach, especially for entry level positions.

Utilize recruitment agencies

There are a growing number of credible recruitment agencies on the African continent with a strong pipeline of potential employees. They typically save the social innovator the difficult job of ploughing through thousands of resumes and conducting physical interviews for numerous candidates. Instead, the recruitment agency presents a shortlist of three to ten candidates as finalists for a position. The cost of utilizing recruitment agencies varies significantly across the continent, but for senior roles, they often require 10 percent to 20 percent of the employee's annual salary. This cost is often prohibitive for African social innovators with limited budgets, who only typically utilize recruitment agencies for highly specialized positions or for senior manager roles that are difficult to fill.

Engage the community

Social innovations gain more local buy-in when they actively recruit individuals from the communities where they work. These individuals understand the language and culture and can easily build trust with community residents and stakeholders. Depending on the level of education and exposure in the community, the management team utilizes a simple advertising and screening tool to identify the most suitable candidates, either for full- or part-time employment, or as entrepreneurs and franchisees. For example, Sanergy, which operates in Kenyan slums, currently utilizes local residents who serve as Fresh Life Operators, and have purchased and are operating the hygienic sanitation facilities. These local operators also recruit other community residents as Fresh Life Frontline, who are trained and properly equipped to remove waste on a daily basis and replace it with clean, empty cartridges. Ninety percent of Sanergy's team members are Kenyans and 60 percent of them reside in the communities they serve. This form of engagement ensures that the organization's impact transcends the innovation they have introduced, and includes employment and training of community residents.

Similarly, Bridge International Academies actively recruits from its local communities. It works closely with community and religious leaders to identify individuals who have had leadership experience in the local church or another community organization and who have strong communication skills. According to Lucy Bradlow at Bridge, 'Our goal is to unlock the talent that has gone unnoticed in the adult population, so that we can change the learning experience of children today'.

Screening talent

In a survey of 1,600[3] businesses across Africa, conducted by McKinsey & Company, over 50 percent of companies cited the scarcity of job-ready candidates as the leading obstacle to hiring new employees. Similarly, social innovators who were interviewed for this book complained that they receive thousands of unsuitable resumes for a few positions and had to engage in very painful screening processes to find one or two gems.

In order to determine a candidate's skills, values and fit within the organizational culture, the management team of high performing organizations typically engage in a tailored screening process, based on the experience and skills required for the role, as stipulated in the job description. For positions with high skill requirements, teams utilize a multi-pronged approach, including resumes, conducting standardized screening tests, case studies and group activities, oral interviews with different members of the team, and on the job observation. A few social innovators utilize the volunteer-to-work system, where individuals are encouraged to join the organization as a volunteer, and are observed over a defined time frame to determine if they can add value and are a good fit within the organization's culture. This typically works best when the individual is unemployed when they are presented for an evaluation. LEAP Africa, a youth and entrepreneur leadership development organization in Nigeria, utilizes this approach to screen potential employees. Consequently, over 40 percent of LEAP's employee base has emerged from this process. Other organizations utilize a training school-to-work system, whereby, based on the results of standardized evaluations, enterprises enroll a number of intakes into a training school for a defined period of time. Recruits are hired as full-time employees based on their performance within the training group, while others are released back into the job market. Riders for Health, which operates across Africa, utilizes this approach to recruit technicians for different vehicle management and maintenance roles, directly contributing to the growing number of skilled mechanics and electricians in the communities. According to the One Acre Fund team, interviewed for this book,

> Field staff interviews are experiential; simulating the actual job being recruited for as much as possible and allowing us to see how candidates would act as One Acre Fund staff members. We often over hire, allowing for the first few months of the job to form an additional testing phase that lets us get to know candidates even better.

For the recruitment of semi-skilled and unskilled workers, social innovators engage key staff in oral interviews and day- or week-long trials and apprenticeships to determine how quickly they can learn and their level of interest and passion. For example, Kidogo, a social enterprise which provides early childhood care for less than $1 per day and operates in the Kibera and Kangemi slums in Kenya, conducts 'practical' interviews for its teachers. This includes observing them interacting with children and interfacing with other teachers.

Throughout the process of attracting and recruiting talent, it is critical that the innovators and their team work diligently to ensure a workforce based on the gender, ethnic and religious balance that reflects the diversity of the community and country. This often takes a concerted effort and requires significantly more emphasis on building a pipeline of those who have a lower representation in the workforce. Often overlooked is also the need to incorporate people with special needs who have the potential to make immense contributions, but are often limited by the lack of basic infrastructure and facilities to enable them to work effectively.

In addition, social innovators with high performing teams institute clear systems and structures to guide the recruitment process, including actively checking references and vetting credentials. They also institute transparent salary, benefits, and bonus structures and terms of employment to ensure a seamless recruitment and retention strategy.

Motivating and retaining talent

As noted earlier, many social innovators cannot match the salaries provided by large corporate organizations or the development community. As a result, they provide other forms of motivation to keep their team members energized and committed to scaling impact. To achieve this goal, they typically offer a bundle of incentives to their employees which include those described below:

BOX 3.2: KEY QUESTIONS FOR INNOVATORS

Do you have a dream team?

- Are your team members passionate about your mission, vision and interventions?
- Do they have the basic credentials and experience for the positions that they occupy?
- Do they have strong communications skills (oral and written)?
- Do they have critical thinking and problem-solving skills?
- Do they have strong technical skills (as required)?
- Do their values and personality fit with the culture of your organization?
- Are they mature? Do they take initiative? Do they have integrity?

Consider utilizing the McKinsey Skill-Will Matrix to assess your team, enabling you to determine which problem areas can be addressed by training and coaching and which group of employees should be disengaged from the organization.

Salaries and benefits

Social innovators that are successfully scaling impact in Africa commit to consistently paying a respectable salary, at the very minimum, with periodic salary increases linked to performance, cost of living adjustments and industry benchmarks. This is critical to engage and retain committed and capable employees. In addition, team members benefit from health insurance and pension schemes and receive bonuses or a 13th month pay out at the end of the year. Sadly, given the struggles with financing scaling, paying decent salaries and benefits remains a challenge for many social entrepreneurs, and some are known to owe employees for many months, leading to high employee turn-over and low productivity.

Equity

This is offered to employees to keep them engaged and deepen their level of ownership and commitment. It is only relevant for social businesses which have shareholders and is typically reserved for those in senior management roles. They can only vest their equity stakes after three to five years of faithful service to the company.

Career path and job responsibility

Every employee benefits from a clear sense of their possible career path within an organization and the stepping stones that the organization would provide to their plans for the future. As a result, it is critical that the social innovator communicates future plans on a periodic basis to team members. In addition, refining the organizational chart, job descriptions, and clarifying the reporting relationships and communicating this to the team enables them to feel more empowered, engaged and challenged to excel and grow with the organization.

Given that most social innovations operate as meritocracies, there are ample opportunities for those who demonstrate a commitment to excellence, team work, and leadership to be given more responsibilities, regardless of their tenure in the organization and what level they occupy. Promotion within the organization is critical, with leading social innovators only recruiting from outside their teams when they need specialized skills or cannot find the in-house expertise. The knowledge that any member of the team could eventually serve as the CEO or Executive Director keeps the team members motivated and committed to growing as individuals in order to assume this role in the future.

Training and coaching talent

Given the skills gaps that often exist among new and current employees, there is also a range of training approaches to meet the unique needs of each group. Most social innovators, given the sheer numbers of talented employees required during periods of scaling, invest in creating extensive in-house training schools to prepare new hires to support their rapid expansion efforts. They also standardize the job functions and utilize very clear operating manuals to guide the team members. Bridge International Academies utilizes technology and tools to reduce the cost and compress the time required for training. The organization has developed its own curriculum, books, and teaching tools which are uploaded to teachers' tablets and uses technology for auditing and data collection.

Other organizations outsource training to business development service providers, local and regional business schools, and international capacity building organizations. Thankfully, there are a growing number of subsidized courses offered by African and global universities for African social innovators and their team members.

Beyond formal training, social innovators also invest in on-the-job training and also provide opportunities for team learning and development. For example, Sanergy, Jobberman, LEAP Africa and AACE Foods hold monthly speaker series and invite external speakers to address topics that are pre-selected by the team. They also invite speakers and trainers to their annual staff retreats. Dimagi, with offices in Senegal and Kenya, provides five personal initiative days for its employees, in addition to their vacation and sick days, to enable them to focus on promoting their own ideas.

Some organizations actively match employees with mentors and/or coaches within or outside the organization through a formal or informal mentoring process. This is a critical tool for engaging team members, enhancing their motivation and improving their productivity.

Task shifting and task sharing

This practice, utilized largely by social innovators in the health and education landscapes, lessens the possibility of burnout and ensures that individuals can seamlessly step in for their colleagues during peak periods. According to Nick Pearson, the founder of Jacaranda,[4]

> We recognize how overworked nurses are around the world, and how difficult it is to provide high quality care when they are spread thin. We focus on task shifting and task sharing to help ensure that clinical expertise falls in the right hands and that human resources are allocated optimally.

Recognition

This is critical to retaining employees, enabling them to feel valued and appreciated. The Paradigm Initiative (PIN), which provides ICT and life skills to youth in Nigeria, utilizes this approach in an innovative manner. It recognizes a 'staff member of the month' – but instead of management nominating this individual at the end of the month, as is the case in most organizations, individuals nominate themselves for this recognition at the beginning of the month at PIN. This individual then has to live up to this designation and act like the best performing staff. The PIN founder, Gbenga Sesan, invests in coaching the staff member of the month, helping them develop a career and life plan as part of this recognition.

Other organizations celebrate individual and team milestones, offer letters of commendation, gifts linked to years of active service, and publicity on the entity's website or publications.

Travel and exposure

Employees value the opportunity to travel to the field to interact directly with the beneficiaries. This is especially relevant for those organizations that have multiple sites, and when their headquarters is far from the impact sites. They also enjoy traveling abroad for defined periods of time to attend conferences, obtain training, or benefit from a study tour to visit another organization engaged in similar activities. Marcela Escobari of the Harvard Kennedy School notes during interview, 'Knowledge travels much faster in brains than into brains', and advocates for the movement of talent between countries to learn, thrive and then return.

Team members appreciate being given ample opportunities to engage in public speaking and media engagements on behalf of the organization. This not only increases the personal recognition that they receive for their service to the organization, but also enhances their sense of pride and ownership. They also typically enjoy representing the organization at key regional, national and international conferences and stakeholder events.

One Acre Fund, which in 2014 had over 2,100 staff, aptly summarizes the approach that enables leading social enterprises to retain capable and committed staff in its white paper on *Professional Development for Field Staff*. According to the team,

> we think retention comes from fair pay, ample development opportunities, and a sense of meaning in work. Meaning comes from giving each staff member a sense of ownership over his or her work. This is combined with a sense of service to their community and other communities. Together, these factors drive long-term retention.

Structuring human resources for scale

Social innovators that are committed to scaling impact recognize that the organizational structure that yielded results in the pilot phase is not suitable for the scale-up phase. Leaning on best practices from large corporations that have scaled across geographies, social enterprises create modular scale-up structures which enable them to reach more beneficiaries exponentially.

Consider the case of Educate! which scaled from serving 54 schools in 2013 to 238 in 2014, and is planning for 350 in 2016. The organization recognized that incrementally adding on one or two schools would prove difficult and expensive. As a result, based on best practices from India, it developed a modular scale-up model, using replicable organizational units. To date Educate! operates this model in two regions. A program coordinator oversees the work of a regional officer, who is responsible for 10 community units. Each community unit has one program officer, supported by one youth leader and together they support six mentors, with each mentor managing three schools. Altogether, there are 18 schools in each community unit and 180 schools in each region. Once these are created, the model begins again at a new location. The key personnel at each layer of the organization is supported by systems, structures, procedures and measurement and evaluation frameworks, to deliver high-impact results at scale. This modular approach will allow Educate! to operate in six regions, eventually working with approximately a third of Ugandan secondary schools across the entire country, as depicted in the Figure 3.1.

Similarly, the One Acre Fund utilizes a district operating unit structure that is scalable. Sixty field officers, who serve approximately 150 farmers, are managed by 10 field managers, who report to a field director. Each One Acre Fund field 'operating unit' can serve approximately 10,000 clients, and every new unit will require the addition of approximately 80 staff in total, composed of field level, field management, and headquarters support employees.

At One Acre's headquarters, each team has specialized roles to support the farmer – who remains the heart of the operations. The procurement team facilitates the purchase and importation of fertilizer in large quantities across its four countries of operation. The logistics team manages warehouses and oversees

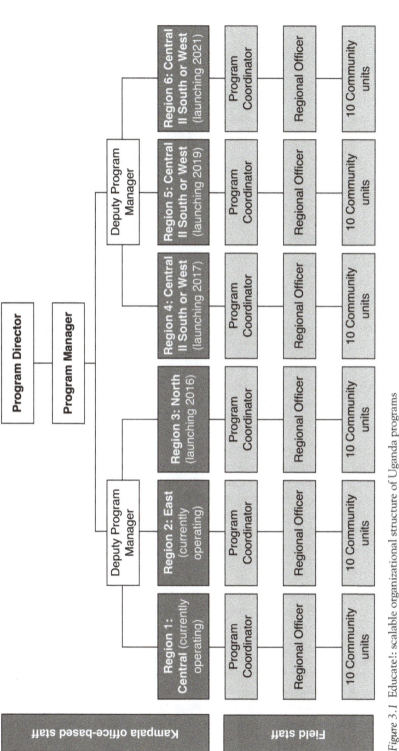

Figure 3.1 Educate!: scalable organizational structure of Uganda programs

Source: Educate! Operation scale overview 2015.

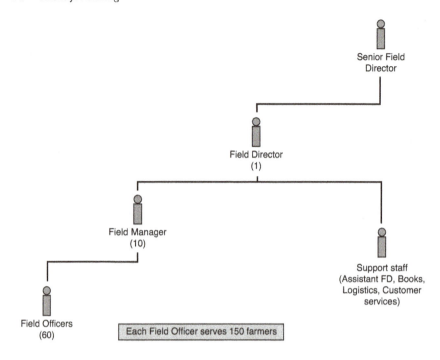

Figure 3.2: One Acre Fund's local staff structure
Source: One Acre Fund interview.

input distribution; and the technology support team develops systems for tracking and analyzing all information related to client orders and repayments.

The examples of Educate! and One Acre reinforce the importance of appropriate organizational design, with clear reporting relationships and distinct roles tied to clear performance indicators for scaling impact.

Beyond the structure, it is imperative that organizations codify their human resources strategy in a manual which is clear, comprehensive and includes the policies, systems, and benefits for its employees, at every level of the organization.

Typically, this manual should include a range of sections. Consider the example from LEAP Africa's human resources manual which includes the following sections:

- **Guiding principles:** This section introduces the organization, outlining its mission, vision and values, its commitment to its employees and its expectations of them. It also explains the company's approach to managing personnel records, provides an overview of the company's ethics, confidentiality and non-compete policies, classification of staff, and policies regarding equal opportunity.

- **Work environment:** This includes information about the entity's hours of operations, policies regarding absences from work, probationary period, prohibitions, dress code, standards of conduct, disciplinary process, disengagement policy and process, cost management approach, environmental policies, internal and external policies, culture and work safety.
- **Leave allowances:** This addresses entitlements for holidays, leave allowances including compassionate leave, sick leave, maternity leave, paternity leave, examination leave and compensatory time.
- **Compensation and performance reviews:** This addresses recruitment processes, promotions, performance review procedures, pay structures and pay periods, taxes and payroll obligations and salary advances.
- **Staff benefits:** This section provides information on pension plans, insurance – including health, life and workers compensation, transport benefit, training, rent subsidies and housing, funeral, survivor, 13th month, bonuses, and other benefits as applicable, loans and leave without pay and membership of professional associations.
- **Reimbursable expenses:** This section outlines the organization's policies on travel and accommodation, transport allowances, travel advances and expense reconciliations, and medical reimbursements.

It is important to recognize that while organizational structures, systems and manuals are critical for aligning employee expectations and setting clear standards of conduct, they are only meaningful if they are implemented and if the senior team leads by example.

Building and sustaining a culture of excellence and innovation

Beyond attracting, recruiting, and retaining committed team members, and designing and implementing effective modular organizational structures, social innovators have to build and sustain a culture of excellence and innovation. This is especially critical during the scaling process, where the founder becomes far removed from the day-to-day management of every employee. This requires being deliberate about measurement and evaluation for employees, and instituting clear systems and structures for sustaining positive aspects of the organization's culture, especially its culture of innovation, ethics, and effective succession management.

Measurement and evaluation

Instituting clear performance measurement systems, linked to quantitative and qualitative results and a 360-degree evaluation – which includes feedback from employees and managers, is critical to motivating employees to perform. Key performance indicators (KPI) linked to the employee's role within the organization, and their contributions to the broader goals of the organization are important tools for motivating employees to perform. Learning and development plans emerge from this biannual evaluation process, which employees can utilize as a guide for the year. High performing social enterprises also provide opportunities for upward feedback, where the employees share improvement opportunities for enhancing the effectiveness and leadership styles of their managers.

Individuals with low performance results who show minimal signs of improvement with support are eventually counseled to exit the organization. Assessing their personal skills, track record within the organization versus their willingness to learn and grow, often clarifies whether they have a future within the organization or not. Ultimately, an organization that is committed to scaling has to build a committed and capable team.

Sustain positive values and culture with scaling

Social innovators have to work diligently to sustain the organization's values and a culture of innovation and continuous improvement, especially during periods of scaling. There are a range of approaches to building this culture which range from in-house creativity and innovation competitions to periodic ideas festivals, where the team invites a range of external collaborators to brainstorm and investigate ideas for improving the organization's service offerings. Regardless of the selected approach, social innovators, who prioritize the importance of sustaining their culture by instituting clear systems and structures, making the time for periodic convenings and providing a space for thinking about continuous improvement, ultimately build high-performing organizations.

Sustaining ethical values is also critical for scaling because it builds trust among all key stakeholders including the community, investors, funders and partners. This can only be achieved by instituting and enforcing systems and structures, boundaries and controls and clear codes of conduct that specifically address issues such as bribery, corruption, conflicts of interest, sexual harassment, discrimination, plagiarism, nepotism and deceit. The leadership, management, and team members must lead by example and exhibit a zero tolerance for unethical behaviour.

Social innovators deliberately leverage every opportunity to reiterate the values and sustain the culture of the organization, especially when it has a wide geographic spread and some employees have little or no direct engagement with the headquarters. Organizations such as Ikamva Youth, which works in three provinces in South Africa, supporting thousands of students in grades 9 to 12 from disadvantaged communities to access tertiary education and/or employment opportunities, maintains an active website with tools, training and information for all its employees and partner organizations. In addition, it has a full-time internal communications team member, whose role is to manage internal information flows and feedback loops to ensure regular information flows across regions and enhance the connectedness and unity of the organization.

Similarly, social ventures such as mPedigree invest in sustaining their culture by creating rings of teams with overlapping leadership structures. Bright Simmons, its founder notes during an interview for this book that the primary roles of the top leadership are mentorship and culture development. According to him,

> the intense focus on hyper-communications internally, and the constant debating and idea sharing creates an almost 'graduate school lab' feel to our operations that makes it very easy for highly smart individuals to convince themselves that they can flourish in the environment and sharpen their edge. We have had a single resignation in more than eight years of operation.

Leverage technology

Technology is being actively utilized to standardize and minimize the cost and time required for training, communications, service delivery, and measurement and evaluation. It is also utilized to minimize the need for expensive expertise. In some communities where innovations are scaling, there are not enough skilled workers to effectively fulfill the organization's mandate, and the use of technology fills the talent deficit, enabling the scaling effort. For example, Viva Afya, a primary health company in Kenya, uses a 'hub-and-spoke' model to serve densely populated, low income areas. The model has a main clinic (hub), which is supported by several electronically connected satellite clinics (spokes). It uses technology to compensate for the lack of qualified skilled health workers by linking registered nurses in satellite clinics electronically to experienced doctors and pharmacists operating at the location hub.

Plan for employee successions

Organizations that scale have to incorporate succession planning into every aspect of their human resources strategy. This concept was best captured by Joy Olivier, the founder of IkamvaYouth in South Africa, who stated, 'We build succession into all the roles within our organization. The more each person's capabilities increases and they can step into the role above, the faster we can scale.' This best practice essentially means that each individual is grooming someone else to step into their role, so that they can move into a more challenging role within the organization. In the case of IkamvaYouth, this may mean setting up a new operation in another province in South Africa or even becoming the next executive director of the organization. Active succession planning, especially for senior management positions, also ensures that the organization is never destabilized or derailed by the sudden exit of a team member. The organization encourages team members to step up to lead growth efforts.

Indeed, by investing in measurement and evaluation, sustaining a culture of innovation and ethics, leveraging technology and planning successions, organizations can ensure that they continue to sustain a culture of excellence and innovation and achieve impact at scale.

Restructuring your team for scaling

Periodically, boards and the management team of any entity attempting to scale have to honestly evaluate their teams to determine whether they have the best people and are structured in the most appropriate way to enable scaling.

Sadly, many of the organizations that are struggling to scale today on the African continent do not have the right people on their teams to achieve the impact at scale they require.

It is never too late to restructure a team. This requires at least five critical steps:

1   *Honestly evaluate the leadership*

Critical evaluations of the leadership start from the founder and his or her commitment to the administrative and managerial tasks associated with scaling. A candid review of the management team often reveals that the skills that enabled an individual to launch a social innovation may not be the ones required to scale that innovation. Too often, the visionary becomes the stumbling block in the scaling process, either because he/she is burnt out from the pilot or would prefer to manage a small entity or grow slowly. If this is the case, a mature leader knows when to step back and let others scale. It is important to recognize that there are numerous ways that a founder who chooses not to personally lead the scaling effort can remain involved in the organization, either as a board member, a major shareholder (in the case of a social venture), or as the chief design officer.

The process of finding a suitable successor is a difficult one, which LEAP Africa has actively covered in two of its popular books – *Passing the Baton* and *Defying the Odds – Case Studies of Nigerian Companies that Have Survived Generations*. However, there are a growing number of successful successions in the African social sector. These organizations typically have strong boards who have led the process of recruiting successors from inside and outside the organizations. The key to their success has been active board engagement, long-term succession planning, honest and open communications with all stakeholders, and a handover period which allows for effective training and support.

BOX 3.3: KEY QUESTIONS FOR INNOVATORS

Are you the best leader to scale social impact?

Do you:

- empower others to lead?
- listen and encourage your team to share positive feedback and constructive criticism?
- communicate regularly – sharing your vision, passion, mistakes and failures?
- invest in measurement and evaluation?

- exhibit honesty and transparency in all of your dealings?
- admit your mistakes and failures and learn from them?
- actively engage others – especially key stakeholders in the community?
- care more about the impact than who gets the glory?
- know when to exit gracefully, and let others scale, if and when you realize that you do not have the skills or interest to take the organization to the next level?

These questions should be used by the innovator to conduct a self-assessment and modified slightly for boards to evaluate the capabilities of the innovator.

2 Based on the redesign of your business model, create a new organizational chart

The business model for scaling that the team adopts will dictate exactly what type of organizational structure would be ideal. If the organization chooses to scale via shaping ecosystems, then it would require a shrinking of the program team, and a new role for a policy and advocacy team. Ultimately, the organizational structure and human resources strategy has to be completely aligned with the business model of the organization in order to enable scaling.

3 Conduct a skills audit of your current team and match it against the new organizational chart

Based on the roles identified and the job descriptions for each role, the management team will need to conduct an in-depth evaluation of the current team members to determine whether they have the requisite skills, experience, and passion for the job. The results of this audit have to be matched against the new organizational chart and the job roles. Similarly, the board will need to periodically review the effectiveness and capabilities of the CEO to determine whether he or she has the skills, passion and values to lead the scaling effort. In some cases the board may decide that the CEO requires additional training and support and may define a capacity building action plan to fill these gaps. In other cases a board may decide that the CEO needs to be replaced and will implement disengagement and new hire recruitment strategies.

4 Hire new blood to fill the gaps and help other team members exit

Based on the skills audit, the management will determine which people need to be moved around the organization, hired to fill new roles or counseled out of the organization. This process is an extremely sensitive one and should be handled with the care and complete respect for the team members who have worked diligently to get the organization to the point of scaling. The management team should actively support them in their job search.

5   Constantly reevaluate the team

Every year, the leadership should reevaluate the team to ensure that it is still well structured to deliver on the mission and vision of the organization.

It is never too late to restructure a team for scaling. By engaging in an honest assessment of the leadership and team's capabilities and interests, against the business model and the needs of the organization, helping some employees to exit and hiring new ones and constantly reevaluating the team's capabilities, the organization can ensure that it is poised for success.

Summary

No social innovation, even one with the best business models, can scale without committed and capable individuals to drive the scaling effort. However, building a dream team with the passion, vision and skills to drive social change is extremely difficult in the African context, given the state of the educational sector, and the multiple opportunities available for the best and brightest. Indeed, organizations that have been able to attract and retain talent for scaling have invested in a credible and capable board of directors, partnerships, leveraged external human resources including volunteers, fellows and short-term consultants, and instituted clear systems and structures for recruiting, retaining and promoting capable employees. They have also invested in designing appropriate scaling structures and restructuring when necessary.

Ultimately, the ability to attract, recruit and retain a team of mission-driven high achievers, and sustain a culture of innovation and excellence, rooted in values, will ensure the scaling of more high-impact innovations on the African continent.

Notes

1   LEAP Africa 2007 *Get on Board: A Practical Guide to Building High-Impact Board of Directors.*

2   *Association internationale des étudiants en sciences économiques et commerciales.*

3   'Winds of change? Building the educational foundations of inclusive growth in Africa', Presentation to Wits Business School Chinezi Chijioke, Education Adviser to McKinsey & Company August 21, 2013.

4   Jacaranda website, accessed April 10, 2015; http://jacarandahealth.org/innovation/

4 Financing scaling

Interviews conducted in 2000 by the Social Investment Task Force in the
United Kingdom, revealed what most nonprofit leaders already know: Almost
all social sector organizations are small and perennially underfunded, with
barely three months' worth of working capital at their disposal.[1]

Financing is cited by innovators operating in Africa as the biggest barrier to
scaling social innovations in the public, private and nonprofit sectors. This
challenge, like many of the others outlined in this book, is not unique to the
African context, as reinforced from the experiences in the UK cited in the quote
above. Innovators operating in Africa often have to contend with a few
additional hurdles including the need to:

- Build linkages to funders, especially those in Europe and the United States,
  who are often removed from the realities of operating in Africa.
- Establish and communicate a strong business case and theory of change,
  backed by sound data that establishes a clear need and sustainable demand.
- Demonstrate credibility from the strength of the founder, board, management
  team, and their track record of integrity, transparency and impact.
- Amplify the impact of their work through creative communication strategies
  to raise broad based awareness and effectively differentiate themselves from
  international NGOs and other key stakeholders.

Innovators who are able to raise significant funds for scaling their social
innovations have to work diligently to overcome these barriers and to develop
innovative approaches for generating funds internally and externally.

This chapter identifies strategies being leveraged by teams that are scaling social
innovations in Africa and emerging trends which should be capitalized upon.

Internally generated funds

As outlined in Chapter 2, social innovations that scale have to utilize demand
driven models. This essentially means that depending on their product or service
offerings and target beneficiaries, they can typically generate some financial

resources. In fact, innovative pricing and payment mechanisms leveraging technology are enabling even the poorest of the poor at the bottom of the pyramid to cover a portion of the costs for the services they receive.

As articulated by Sally R. Osberg and Roger Martin in their May 2015 HBR article, sustainable social enterprises, must also be financially sustainable. Otherwise the new socioeconomic equilibrium will require a constant flow of subsidies from taxpayers or charitable givers, which are difficult to guarantee indefinitely. To achieve sustainability, an enterprise's costs should fall as the number of its beneficiaries rises, allowing the venture to reduce its dependence on philanthropic or governmental support as it grows.[2]

In the African context, more social innovators are generating revenue from fee for service via cross subsidization, pay as you go, and contracts for outsourced services. Others are generating investment income from strategic investments and endowments.

Fee for service

Cross subsidization

This describes business models where support for one product or service comes from revenues generated from another product or service. There are three typical forms of cross-subsidization which are being utilized by social innovators, as outlined in the May 2015 SSIR article titled 'Investing in cross-subsidy for greater impact':[3]

- Offer a standardized product or service to all customers or clients, with differential pricing based on customer type or ability to pay. For example: the Children's Development Center (CDC) in Lagos Nigeria, a nonprofit educational centre that caters to children with special needs, offers the same high quality care to all children, based on a sliding fee scale linked to household income.
- Offer a higher-priced upgraded product to cover the cost of providing discounted or free products. For example, d.light, a social enterprise which provides solar energy solutions for households and small businesses, subsidizes more basic products for low-income customers but also sells higher-end products. Since its inception in 2006, d.light has sold 10 million products in 62 countries with the goal of transforming the lives of 100 million people by 2020.[4]
  - Similarly, Jobberman, the second largest job placement website in Africa, listed as one of The World's Top 10 Most Innovative Companies of 2015 in Africa, offers a tiered pricing structure. According to correspondence with Ayodeji Adewunmi, the President and CEO of Jobberman 'Our pricing is tiered and allows for varied organizations irrespective of size, micro enterprises to multinationals, to utilize the products and services on the platform allowing the platform to do business with 45,000+ companies'.

- MPedigree also utilizes this approach, by convincing manufacturers and distributors to pay for its software and inbed its technology into their product packaging and supply chain. This enables the companies to manage the entire end-to-end transformation, administrative, and operational process, while the consumers and retailers of their products obtain the product: 'quality authentication service' for free. Correspondence with Bright Simmons, the founder of MPedigree detailed, 'we are impacting more than 50 million people and protecting more than 500 million units of life-touching consumables. We now have activities in over a dozen countries and industries'.
- Offer different products and rely on one product to subsidize the other. Some technology hubs such as MEST in Accra, Bongohive in Lusaka, the Co-Creation Hub in Lagos or the more than 90 hubs operating across Africa, offer software, website development and consulting services to enable them to offer free work space and other support services to aspiring entrepreneurs. They also rent out their open spaces for community programs and business plan competitions.

Pay-as-you-go

This approach specifically caters to the bottom of the pyramid (BOP) populations, enabling them to pay per use, as opposed to having to commit their limited resources in advance of receiving the services or products required. The emergence of M-Pesa and other mobile payment systems across Africa has facilitated the pay as you go model, especially among providers of off-grid energy solutions. For example, M-KOPA, which operates in Kenya, Uganda and Tanzania, serving over 200,000 households, utilizes a pay-per-use installment plan. Customers acquire solar systems for a small deposit of $35 and then purchase daily usage 'credits' for US $0.45, significantly less than the price of traditional kerosene lighting. After one year of payments, customers own their solar systems and can upgrade to more power.

Similarly, Kidogo operates early childhood education centres in slum communities in Kenya which cater to women who earn daily or weekly wages. These women pay $1 per day to obtain high quality care and education for their children. Parents receive slight discounts when they pay in advance for a week of care.

Unbundling

This essentially refers to a pricing methodology that breaks down the product or service into component parts which then empowers the customer to determine which particular component is more important at a given time, and which to pay for based on their needs. This is particularly relevant in the healthcare setting, where clients can pay for doctor's visits, lab tests and medicine.

There is often a debate in the social sector about whether low income and vulnerable populations should contribute financially to the services that they receive from a social innovator. There are strong opinions on both ends of the spectrum – with many arguing for some very small financial contribution to increase the commitment and expectations of the beneficiary. For example, Educate! which delivers a skills-based education model for students in Ugandan high schools, requires that its partner schools contribute towards the training and support on a sliding scale. School contributions provide only about 1 percent of the overall budget of Educate! However, this aligns the needs of the major stakeholders and enhances the ownership of the teams in the schools.

Contractors for key stakeholders

Some social innovators establish their innovation and the organization that hosts it as service providers for governments or a private sector initiative. This enables them to generate income via contracts or payments linked directly to the service that they provide. For example, Riders for Health, an international, not-for-profit social enterprise works across Africa, providing transportation and logistics services typically for Ministries of Health, enabling them to reach the rural and underserved communities. Riders manages and maintains fleets of vehicles for the government and is paid for this service. On average, 60 percent[5] of its revenue is generated from contracts with African governments and development sector clients.

Other income

Social innovators who serve low-income and vulnerable populations recognize the limits to their ability to utilize the fee-for-service model. This is especially difficult when their target populations need the service or product but cannot afford it or do not perceive the immediate value. Examples of these types of services include voter education, nutrition awareness, civic education, shelters for abused women, and healthcare services for internally displaced people. In order to provide high-impact products and services to meet these needs, organizations in Africa are increasingly developing other avenues for generating income.

For example, ActionHealth Incorporated (AHI) Nigeria, an award-winning, youth-focused, reproductive health nonprofit, established AHI Residences, an 18-bed hotel, which allows the organization to save costs during its residential training program for educators and also enables it to generate revenue to offset some of its operating expenses. In addition, AHI attracts income by providing training, selling its books and publications and offering consultancy services.

It is important to recognize that it is easy for social innovators to get side tracked and consumed by their need to generate income, losing sight of their social mission in the process. In order to avoid this trap, social innovators who are committed to scaling social impact must have a clear mission and vision, governance structures and periodic checks to ensure that they remain focused. They also should attempt to generate income via mechanisms that are closely aligned to their mission and objectives. For example, instead of operating a bakery to generate income, LEAP Africa sells books on a range of management and leadership topics to the general public through book shops, targeted events and via websites. These books are already an important component of LEAP's core training programs; however, the ability to sell the books to thousands of entrepreneurs enables the organization to generate additional income, while still making an impact.

The importance of a strong connection between an organization's mission and its need to generate earned income was clearly articulated by Afzal Habib, Chief Imagination Officer at Kidogo.

> We have to make our business more financially sustainable and subsidize the cost of running low-cost centers that are unprofitable. As a result, we are exploring new revenue streams such as microfranchising, publishing, consulting, clothing and retail – all related to our core focus on early childhood education.

Achieving financial self-sufficiency

Every social entrepreneur's dream is to build an organization that is economically self-sufficient. Sadly, this goal appears elusive for most social innovators on the African continent. However, while difficult, this goal is achievable, and requires at least three critical steps.

The first step to achieving self-sufficiency is to **actively track the self-sufficiency metric and ensure accurate financial management systems** to validate the accuracy of the costs and revenue generated by the organization. One Acre Fund actively tracks its financial sustainability metric – defined as the percentage of its field operating costs – the cost of farm inputs, field salaries, logistics costs, and administrative support that is covered by farmer repayment. As depicted in the table below, the organization has been able to make significant gains, especially in its first six years of operations. These gains were largely linked to economies of scale. By engaging more farmers, One Acre Fund was able to obtain better prices from major input suppliers and utilize existing staffing to meet its needs.

Financial data from the field feeds into the overall sustainability ratio. More specifically, the organization tracks revenue per client, costs of goods sold to the client and the gross margin per client across the board.

These results indicate profits at the 'gross margin per field officer' level. However, these are allocated to cover the shared costs at the regional, national and international levels that provide support to field operations, resulting in the 78 percent financial sustainability ratio in 2014. Invariably, the organization still depends on donors to cover the balance of funds that it requires.

However, by actively tracking these ratios, the organization can develop strategies for driving improvements, and reducing dependency.

The second step is to **actively manage costs**. One Acre Fund has imbibed this tenet and actively examines key cost items to determine how to reduce them,

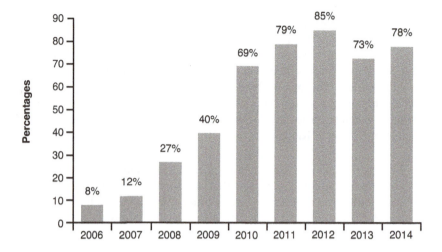

Figure 4.1 One Acre Fund's financial sustainability

Source: One Acre Fund, 'Driving financial sustainability', White Paper, December 2014.

including inculcating a culture of efficiency and cost savings at all levels of the organization. The reality on the continent is that there are numerous ways to reduce administrative expenses, but limited emphasis at the company level to achieve this. Leveraging economies of scale and ensuring that costs decline as the entity reaches and serves more people is critical.

The third step is to **increase revenue**, utilizing all of the strategies outlined in the section above. This requires considerable creativity, tenacity and flexibility, to find avenues for generating additional earned income, while sustaining the focus of the organization on addressing the social mission for which it was established. In the case of One Acre Fund, field teams offer farmers a range of crop packages for staples such as maize and beans, including fertilizer, seeds, training and insurance. It also offers ancillary products such as solar lights and tree planting kits. Ultimately, its products and services are aligned with its mission and

Table 4.1 Field officer economics by country 2014

	Kenya	Rwanda	Burundi
Clients per field officer	121	143	219
Revenue per client	$88	$75	$42
Cost of good per client	$56	$55	$29
Gross margin per client	$32	$20	$13
Gross margin per field officer	$3,872	$2,860	$2,847

Source: One Acre Fund, 'Driving financial sustainability', White Paper, December 2014.

objectives and the farmers have a choice as to whether to partner with One Acre Fund or to leverage an alternate support structure.

Indeed, there is a fine line between supporting and exploiting the lowest income populations, and social innovators need to carefully straddle this thin line, ensuring that it is never crossed. Ultimately, organizations that are able to actively track their costs and reduce them and increase revenue will achieve financial self-sustainability.

Externally generated funds

Many social innovations have to depend on externally generated funds in the first few years of the pilot and scaling process. Others are dependent on external funding in the long term. This dependency is linked to the business model of the innovation, its target customer and client base and the ability of the social entrepreneur to generate sufficient earned income to cover its operating expenses at scale. Since 2000, there has been a growing number of funding sources available to social innovators on the African continent, including donations and grants, challenge funds, fellowships, competitions and prizes, impact investments, social impact bonds and crowd funding.

Donations and grants

These essentially refer to funds that are provided to an entity at no cost to the organization and with no expectation that the organization would have to return the funds, unless they are no longer needed. The major difference between a donation and a grant is the concept of administration.

Donations are typically provided by individuals and companies, either solicited or unsolicited, to support a cause, without the burden of reporting on each aspect of the implementation and use of funds. However, reporting always helps increase the credibility of the organization and promotes referrals to new donors.

A grant is linked to a direct program or project and the beneficiary is expected to report on the impact achieved. There are typically two forms of grants: restricted – which refers to funds specifically earmarked for key activities, which explicitly have to be accounted for and reported upon. In the event that the funds are not needed for what they were initially requested, they would either be returned to the funder or re-allocated to another activity, following a formal request from the grantee. Unrestricted funds are donations that are available for the organization to use towards any purpose.

There are a growing number of foundations operating on the African continent which provide grants to social innovators. The Ford and Rockefeller Foundations provided grants for many of the earliest innovations and social change projects in Africa. For example, The Ford Foundation made its first grant in South Africa in 1954 to support exchange programs in education, business and journalism. In the 1980s, it provided grants to create a network of international and South African legal experts who challenged the legal basis for apartheid and were central participants in shaping the new constitution. In addition, The International Institute of Tropical Agriculture (IITA) was established in 1967 in Ibadan, Nigeria with funding from the Nigerian government, Rockefeller and the Ford Foundation. IITA has emerged as a leading centre for research on new crop varieties and a critical stakeholder in the global green revolution.

Funders operating on the African continent include personal and corporate foundations, operating and grant-making foundation and diplomatic offices and development agencies. There are significant variations in the regional focus of many of these funders, with the majority concentrating their efforts in specific countries and focusing on specific sectors. In addition to the large global foundations such as the Bill & Melinda Gates Foundation, MacArthur Foundation and the Open Society Institute, there are a growing number of indigenous personal and corporate foundations established by Africans to support social innovators on the continent. In Nigeria alone, over 50 foundations have emerged over the past 15 years, including the Christopher Kolade Foundation, Dangote Foundation, the FATE Foundation, the MTN Foundation, the Tony Elumelu Foundation, the TY Danjuma Foundation and the UBA Foundation. However, many of them are operating foundations which means that they design and deliver programs directly, with only a few grant making foundations providing funding for social innovators to utilize to launch or scale social innovations.

Sizeable individual giving from Africans for social innovations is still in its infancy, primarily because there are no tax incentives to propel this movement, and many Africans already give significant amounts of money to their immediate and extended family members, local churches or mosques, and actively support community activities.

It is important to recognize that while the availability of grants is important in the African context for innovators looking to scale, there are a few critical drawbacks. First, grants can often sidetrack the social innovator from their key focus and business model. As discussed in Chapter 2, 'Sustainable business models that scale', donors often provide sizeable amounts of funds for predefined programs and projects which do not directly match the initiative's mission and vision of the social change agenda. In order to avoid this temptation, social innovators have to be willing and able to decline funds that do not directly fit their programmatic needs. Second, foundations are often reluctant to provide core organizational funding which covers overhead or administrative expenses. In rare cases where they agree to cover these expenses, they are typically unwilling to contribute more than 20 percent of overall project expenses towards overhead or administrative expenses.

According to Christy Chen of The Draper Richards Kaplan Foundation, the challenge with grants is that the majority of them are 'pay for performance contracts'. The funder often provides just enough to implement, with no money to grow, evaluate or plan. Social innovators need additional risk capital so that they can experiment, and patient capital, which is essentially long-term financing, which does not put them under undue pressure to repay immediately. Clearly, this approach limits social innovators and their teams.

In-kind support

Beyond financial contributions as donations and grants, social enterprises also benefit from a range of products and services which are offered at significant discounts or for free. These contributions include volunteer time, discounts on media advertising and bank fees, free airline tickets, books and even office space. They should always be costed at market rates and actively tracked as an important source of support for the organization.

Consider the experience of mPedigree. According to its founder, Bright Simmons in correspondence,

> since we had no external investment from the outset, and raising capital appeared virtually impossible, we capitalized our operations with 'support in kind'. We partnered with major corporations, but never from the CSR angle but more from their research and development or 'innovation' wings.

mPedigree received significant pro-bono legal support and in-kind private sector support from Orange, HP, Xerox, Vodafone, MTN and many others. The company also partnered with government agencies in Nigeria and Kenya, and major health professional associations.

Challenge funds

These funds are emerging as a key financing source for social innovators in the private, public and nonprofit sectors. They are often established by development partners and foundations and are typically announced and processed via funding windows with clear guidelines, timelines and steps for applications. Typically, innovators have to demonstrate social impact and an ability to contribute a portion of the costs required for the scaling process. One example of a high-impact challenge fund on the African Continent is the Africa Enterprise Challenge Fund (AECF) funded by the UK Department for International Development (DFID). Operating from 2008 to date, AECF[6] has held 18 funding competitions, and allocated approximately US$244 million to 208 private sector companies. This funding which is expected to be matched by the companies serves as a catalyst for initiatives in the agriculture landscape with a focus on practical projects that are both commercially viable and have a broad developmental impact on the rural poor.

Another challenge fund is Innovations Against Poverty,[7] funded by the Swedish International Development Cooperation Agency (SIDA), which propels the private sector to develop products, services and business models that can contribute to poverty reduction and combat climate change. In addition, the TradeMark East Africa Challenge Fund is focused on promoting cross-border trade in East Africa ultimately to boost trade and stimulate economic growth in the region.[8]

Fellowships

These have supported the emergence of several social innovators on the continent through multi-sector initiatives targeted at providing start-up funding, customized support services, executive education and advisory services. They include fellowships offered by the Acumen Fund, Ashoka,[9] Echoing Green, Transparency International's Social Entrepreneurs Initiative for West Africa, Schwab Foundation for Social Entrepreneurship, Skoll, Draper Richards Kaplan Foundation, Stanford's SEED Program and the Rockefeller Foundation. Some of these fellowships specifically provide financial support for the social innovator for a defined period of time, covering a portion or all of his or her salary to enable the social innovator to focus exclusively on implementing their vision and scaling their innovation. Senegalese born, Lobe Cissokho is an Ashoka Fellow. Her social enterprise, Mutuelle de Sante Oyofal Paj de Kaolack seeks to tackle the problem of rural poverty and unaffordable healthcare costs for women. Working with partners such as Family Health International (FHI), the United States Agency for International Development (USAID), mutual credit and savings institutions and health insurance mutual institutions, her organization provides comprehensive health insurance for as low as $0.35 per person per month. It currently caters to 5,000 direct beneficiaries and 49,000 indirect beneficiaries and has a budget of just under $2 million.

Competitions, prizes and awards

These are also emerging as useful sources of additional growth funding for social innovators. Several funding organizations, foundations and development partners have introduced competitions such as Agribiz4Africa and SheLeadsAfrica to encourage youth entrepreneurs and promote social innovation. In addition, awards such as Innovation Prize for Africa (IPA), Hivos Social Innovation Awards, D-Prize, EMRC Project Incubator Award, Omidyar Network, and African Leadership Network are available for social innovators. While some of these prizes are global in nature, they have started making a concerted effort to incorporate African Social Innovators, with a few specifically targeting breakthroughs in health, agriculture, education and energy.

Companies with operations on the African continent are adding on specific social entrepreneur prizes to existing or new award competitions and ceremonies. These include Unilever's Sustainable Living Young Entrepreneurs Awards and Sustainability Entrepreneur Prize, Ernst & Young's Social Entrepreneurship Awards, and the Orange African Social Venture Prize.

Impact investment

Defined by the Rockefeller Foundation[10] as 'investments intended to create positive impact beyond financial returns', impact investments are a growing source of financing for scaling in Africa. Acumen Fund, Omidyar and Root Capital are early movers in this arena. Other active players include Novaster, Grassroots

Business Fund, Legatum, LGTVP, Lundin, Village Capital and Pearson with its Pearson Affordable Learning Fund. In addition, development partners such as USAID, DFID and the Dutch government have established funds which invest directly or via other venture capital or private equity vehicles.

A 2015 study conducted by JP Morgan and the Global Impact Investing Network (GIIN) estimated that the size of the impact investment landscape is $60 billion, with over 70 percent for emerging markets.[11] Fourteen percent of this funding is being channeled to sub-Saharan Africa, which has the second largest fund allocation in terms of regional spread after North America. At last count, more than 60 impact investment funds and other investment vehicles have a presence in Nairobi, Kenya, where few existed 15 years ago.

Beyond the financial returns generated from investments, these investors actively track impact, with significant variations on how exactly this is defined. For example, some development institutions examine the number of low-income and female beneficiaries and the net employment generated, others assess changes in the livelihoods of the rural poor, and move beyond employment to gauge job sustainability and improvements in quality of life.

Despite the growth in the number of impact investors engaging in the African continent, and the positive returns realized by fund managers, many investors flock to the same 'investee darlings', who typically have strong ties abroad. In their defence, the impact investors complain about the challenges associated with finding 'investment-ready' companies with strong financial track records and governance structures. They also note that there are high costs associated with completing due diligence on transactions and significant lead time to complete the process. They also complain about the difficulties associated with exiting invest-ments after three to seven years, primarily because there is no second tier investor market to buy them out. In addition, in recent years, some investors have explained that the value of their investments have been eroded due to the unstable micro and macroeconomic policies and rapid currency devaluations in Ghana, Nigeria and South Africa.

BOX 4.1: QUESTIONS FOR SOCIAL INNOVATORS

Is your company investment ready?

- Are you recognized as an innovative, credible and accountable leader, with an experienced and committed team?
- Do you have a positive track record based on what else the team has done prior to or through this intervention?
- Do you have strong governance structures, including a committed board that the investor can work with?
- Do you have proven market opportunity? Do you have a solid business model?

- Can you demonstrate evidence of a healthy business: strong financial management systems and positive cash flow, and the potential for an attractive upside for the impact investment?
- Can you demonstrate a feasible exit?
- What strategies do you have to mitigate the biggest environmental, social and economic risks associated with the innovation?

Social impact bonds (SIBs)

Also described as 'pay for success' instruments, social impact bonds are increasingly becoming popular tools for large scale social interventions. Initially piloted by Social Finance in the UK, it involves raising risk capital from private investors to pilot a social intervention. According to Jane Newman, the International Director at Social Finance,

> SIBs are innovative financing instruments that are designed to help govern-ments explore and expand effective social programmes among a pre-defined target group. They bring rigor, innovation and flexibility to social programmes by focusing on pre-set outcomes, testing new innovations and building responsive programmes that are managed to deliver the best results.[12]

Outcome funders commit to repay the capital plus returns to the private investor only if the intervention successfully meets pre-determined outcome and output metrics. A 2015 study by the Brookings Institute[13] reviewed 44 SIBs which are being utilized to address a range of social issues, largely in the United Kingdom and the United States, focused on providing high-quality preschool education, reducing prison recidivism, avoiding foster care placement, and increasing youth employment. This study revealed that while SIBs were effective in driving social innovations and engaging a wide range of partners, they were less effective in terms of reach. Instead, they served as catalysts by encouraging governments to take on the funding or service provision of a proven high impact intervention beyond the life of the bond.

DCapital, a subsidiary of Dalberg, is piloting a malaria impact bond in Mozambique, the first of its kind in Africa. The bond, called 'the Mozambique Malaria Performance Bond (MPPB)' is structured to last over a period of 10 years. It focuses on the Maputo province of Mozambique and aims to reduce malaria prevalence in the area by up to 75 percent. The bond has raised money from private investors and the proceeds of the fundraising process are being used for an integrated malaria control program through annual disbursements over a period of 12 years. If the effort is successful, bond investors will get a 5 percent return. If it is not, they will only get back 50 percent of their initial capital. Entities that stand to benefit from the eradication of malaria in Mozambique, such as the government, mining corporations and public donors are expected to fund the repayment of the capital and returns to initial investors. Already, Nandos, a restaurant chain, has partnered with DCapital in the development of the bond.

Crowdfunding

This practice of funding a project or venture by raising financial contributions from a large number of people, typically via the internet is gaining popularity on the African continent.

There are two main models or types of crowdfunding. The first is called the donation-based funding, where funders contribute via a collaborative goal based process in return for products, perks or rewards. The second and more recent model is investment crowdfunding, where businesses seeking capital sell stakes online in the form of equity or debt. In this model, individuals who contribute become owners or shareholders and have a potential for financial return, unlike in the donation model.

According to the July 2015 AlliedCrowds 2nd Quarter Report, Kenya is Africa's leading nation in terms of money raised via crowdfunding, and the fourth in the developing world. Propelled by its 52.3 percent[14] internet penetration and large mobile payment industry, the country has been at the forefront of crowdfunding, with $15.3 million projected for the year. AlliedCrowds notes that the 'majority (71 percent) of Kenya's crowdfunding activity is via lending platforms, with international P2P lenders Kiva and Zidisha making up roughly 77 percent of the market share in the country'.[15] There are also some emerging sites dedicated exclusively to countries or projects on the African continent. For example, M-Changa, based in Kenya, allows individuals to raise money from their immediate community, in the traditional Kenyan spirit of *harambee*,[16] for social causes, and personal needs. It uses an SMS service to help promote and remind friends and backers of the active projects. The funds can be donated free of charge via mobile money, with the company charging only the recipient a fee of 4.25 percent of the total money raised.

Tomato Jos, a social venture focused on tomato farming and processing in Northern Nigeria, raised $50,000 in 2014 from Kickstarter via a compelling video on the high post-harvest losses associated with tomato, and the dependency of the country on imported paste. They used the donation-based model, offering contributors different gifts including tomato paste and spices for their contributions. However, the exposure that the campaign generated also enabled the founders, Mira Mehta and Shane Kiernan, to attract venture capital and they are currently actively engaged in the process of raising additional funds.

Nonprofits operating in Africa have also successfully used crowdfunding campaigns. For example, according to Otto Orondaam, the founder of Slum2School in an interview for this book,

> From inception our most innovative financial strategy and major source of fundraising has always been our annual crowd fundraising campaign, which

Table 4.2 The five leading global crowdsourcing sites, as ranked by Forbes in 2013

Platform	Model
Kickstarter	Donations
Indiegogo	Donations
Crowdfunder	Investment
Rocket Hub	Donations
Crowdrise	Donations

Source: Barnett, Chance 2013 'Top 10 Crowdfunding Sites For Fundraising', *Forbes*, May 8, 2013; www.forbes.com/sites/chancebarnett/2013/05/08/top-10-crowdfunding-sites-for-fundraising/2/

is organized every summer using social media, and driven by our network of volunteers. This model has proven to be very effective as it not only enables us to raise funds, but also engages our volunteers as brand ambassadors, and helps us create awareness. Since the first social media fundraising campaign in 2012 over ₦12 million (Naira) has been raised collectively from over 500 individual donations.

There are a few features of the crowdfunding process which social innovators should recognize:

Fees

The crowdfunding sites often charge a fee for hosting the campaign, which is typically between 5 and 15 percent of the money raised. Sites also charge a payment-processing fee of approximately 3 percent, although some companies require that the initiator uses a service such as PayPal, in which case that fee goes to PayPal. Some sites transfer funds directly to a designated bank account at no additional fee.

All or nothing

Some crowdfunding sites provide everything that is raised to the social innovator, less the financing charges, regardless of whether or not the innovator meets his or her pre-stipulated target. Others opt to keep the funds raised, if the innovator does not meet his/her target.

The first and largest crowdfunding community for nonprofits in the global arena is called GlobalGiving,[17] which since 2002 has raised close to 200 million dollars from approximately 493,000 donors who have supported 13,213 projects.

Loans

Social enterprises and nonprofits in the African context, like many other small and medium-sized enterprises, rarely consider loans, given the short-term options and double-digit interest rates offered by most financial institutions. However, the landscape is changing and financial institutions are becoming more progressive, especially with pressure on them by central banks to offer more tailored services. One rare example of an innovative loan financing model was designed by Riders for Health in 2009, when it leveraged an investment of $3.5 million[18] to implement a national-scale transport asset management (TAM) program in the Gambia. This financing was obtained in the form of a loan over five years from Guaranty Trust (GT) Bank and was underwritten by the Skoll Foundation. It enabled Riders to purchase a fleet of 210 motorcycles and four-wheeled vehicles, including 35 trekking vehicles, 57 ambulances and 12 multi-purpose vehicles.

As a result of this investment, the Gambia has become the first African country with an appropriate number of health care delivery vehicles for the size of its population and for the structure of its health system. This in turn has strengthened

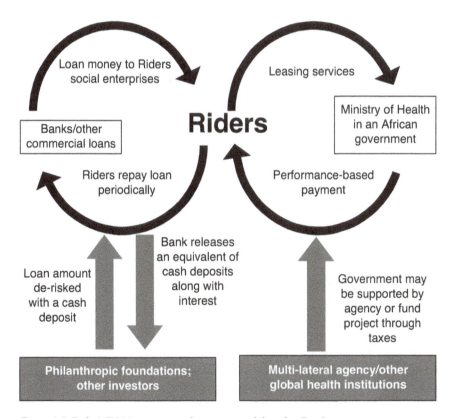

Figure 4.2 Rider's TAM innovative financing model in the Gambia

Source: 'Riders' PPP model: innovation in pricing and capital finance', 5th International Social Innovation Research Conference, ISIRC, September 2013 Saïd Business School, University of Oxford.

the entire healthcare system, ensuring that more rural poor households have access to quality healthcare services.

Clearly Guaranty Trust Bank has served as a pioneer in this regard and other banks need to take the bold step to support more social innovations.

Public sector funding

Unlike the United States, where the government is the largest funder of programmes in the education, health, agriculture and sanitation sectors, this is often not the case in Africa. In reality, social innovators operating in Africa complain that the government often serves as a deterrent or competitor, instead of a partner to scale high impact initiatives. However, there are some positive examples of public sector funding for innovations in the agriculture, health, education and energy sectors which are worthy of recognition.

For instance, in 2014, the Federal Ministry of Agriculture and Rural Development in Nigeria in 2014 partnered with KFW, the German Development Bank, to launch the Fund for Agricultural Finance in Nigeria (FAFIN). It is an innovative agriculture-focused investment fund that provides tailored capital and technical assistance solutions to commercially-viable small and medium-sized enterprises (SMEs) and intermediaries across the agricultural sector in Nigeria using quasi-equity, equity and debt instruments to structure investments. The Nigerian Sovereign Wealth Authority has also invested in the Fund and Sahel Capital serves as the fund manager.

Similarly, at the state-level, following five years of a DFID-funded Education Sector Support Program in Nigeria (ESSPIN), three state governments collectively contributed in $20.5 million between 2012 and 2014 to scale this high-impact program.

These two landmark interventions demonstrated the potential of the government as a funding partner for scaling social innovations on the African continent. Far from easy, strategies for engaging with the government are explored in detail in Chapter 5.

Steps to raise funding

As outlined above, there are numerous funding sources for social innovators to consider. However, the process of raising funding from these sources is difficult and demands a proactive fundraising strategy. There are four critical steps to achieve the desired results:

1   Determine your need for funds and appetite for the options available.
2   Determine if your entity is investment ready.
3   Reach out, engage, negotiate and accept.
4   Implement, measure, monitor and report.

Table 4.3 Spectrum of funding options for different stakeholders

Structure		Nonprofit	For-profit	Hybrid	Public sector
Possible sources of funding	Internal	Fee for service Cross subsidization and Returns on investments	Fee for service Cross subsidization and Returns on investments	Fee for service Cross subsidization and Returns on investments	Fee for service Cross subsidization and Returns on investments
	External	Friends and family Donations and grants Challenge funds Competitions/awards/prizes Crowdfunding Social impact bonds	Friends and family Grants Competitions/awards/prizes Challenge funds Crowdfunding Loans Private equity Social impact bonds	Friends and family Donations and grants Competitions/awards/prizes Challenge funds Crowdfunding Loans Private equity Social impact bonds	Donations and grants Challenge funds Loans
Key questions to consider		Will this initiative require a subsidy for its lifespan because the type of beneficiaries it serves cannot pay market rates or does not immediately value the product or service?	How much money does the social venture require? How much engagement or support does the entity require from external investors? Will the organization break even and generate returns for investors or be positioned to pay back loans? Is the organization investment ready?	Can operations be segmented neatly into a for-profit and nonprofit component, either incorporated in different countries or into distinct entities which allow the social innovator to take advantage of the funding sources that are available for the different structures?	How much funding does the government need to scale a social innovation? Which partners are interested in supporting the government to achieve impact?

Determine your need for funds and appetite for the options available

The management team has to determine exactly what amount of internal or external funding is required, the purpose of the funding, and what sources of funding are available to them. Their structure, stage in the growth process, credibility and linkages will define to a large extent which pools of funding they can leverage, as outlined in table 4.3.

Consider the case of Sanergy which operates a hybrid, a nonprofit and a for-profit, each of which is uniquely dependent on the other for its sustained existence. Under this hybrid structure, the for-profit develops and scales up capital-intensive sanitation technology and infrastructure, and the nonprofit supports sanitation infrastructure and services within low-income communities. Reflecting on this structure, David Auerbach, Sanergy's co-founder, noted: 'we've found that grant funders are comfortble with the social mission priorities in the nonprofit, and that investors like the fact that we cannot fulfill our financial goals without actually providing hygienic sanitation. Both are inextricably linked.'[19]

Determine if your entity is investment ready

As outlined above, external funders are only interested in engaging with organizations that have strong credibility, governance structures, financial management systems and controls and can demonstrate the ability to utilize the funds to achieve results.

In fact, impact investors and foundations complain that many of the organizations in their pipeline are not investment ready. To ensure that their organizations are investment ready, social innovators should actively address the issues raised in Box 4.1, page 75, by following these guidelines:

- Institute a strong board, composed of credible and capable independents and hold regular board meetings.
- Build a strong management team, and establish a robust human resource strategy which enables the innovator to demonstrate that his/her entity is an institution which runs effectively, whether or not the founder or social innovator is present.
- Develop and demonstrate a clear and comprehensive strategy for scaling a sound business model which is demand driven, low-cost, simple, with clear performance management systems and structures.
- Institute clear financial management systems, regular external audits, boundaries and controls, and financial reports that demonstrate that the organization is healthy. Key financial reports and controls that investors expect to see actively utilized within an organization include:
  - **budgets**: annual and quarterly budgets which enable financial planning and monitoring;
  - **balance sheets**: these lay out the assets and liabilities of the entity at a particular date in a calendar year, and allow the entity to understand its financial position;

- **profit and loss statements:** enable the leadership to understand the results of operations, sources of earnings, cost drivers and profitability;
- **cash flow statements:** provide insights into the inflow and outflow of funds into the entity to meet its needs;
- **financial snapshots:** summarize key performance indicators based on financial objectives.

To actively monitor its financial health an organization must have a chief financial officer, or at the very least a strong accountant, suitable accounting software and annual external audits.

Reach out, engage, negotiate and accept

African social innovators often remain isolated in their circles of trust, without strong networks locally, regionally and internationally. In reality, social innovators who require financing for scaling have to step outside of their comfort zones to build linkages across industries and borders. They also have to increase their visibility and profiles to attract funding partners. In order to access funding in the United States, some social innovators have registered their organizations either as a private entity or as a nonprofit, with 501(C)3 status, which requires compliance with reporting requirements of state and federal tax authorities.

Consider the One Acre Fund experience in fundraising, from its inception in 2006 to 2015. Andrew Youn's fundraising journey from life as an MBA student at Kellogg School of Management to an award-winning social entrepreneur is very instructive:

Table 4.4 One Acre Fund's fundraising trajectory

Date	Funder	Amount
April 2006	Yale Business Plan Competition – Social Entrepreneurship Track	$50,000
May 2006	Echoing Green Scholarship	Two-year stipend
2007	Draper Richard Kaplan Foundation	$300,000 (spread over three years)
2007	Mulago Social Investments	$100,000
2009–2010	Pershing Square Foundation	$6.5M (directed into the permanent fund which provides basic capital for loans to farmers)
2010	Skoll Foundation	$750,000
2011–2015	Mastercard Foundation	$10M
	Bill & Melinda Gates Foundation	$11.6M (subsequent grants have been provided)
	Kiva	$4.4 million in loans for its farmers

Source: One Acre website; accessed August 2 2015; www.oneacrefund.org/blogs; http://site.one acrefund.org/about_us/awards_recognition.

Similar to One Acre Fund, Off-Grid Electric in Tanzania, M-Kopa, Sanergy, Bridge International Academies and Jacaranda in Kenya, have also attracted significant financing over the past ten years, especially for scaling. While on face value it may appear that they may be receiving some preferential treatment from international funders, given their strong links to the United States, it is important to note that they have imbibed many of the principles outlined in this book. They constantly extend themselves through partnerships and networks, enhancing their visibility, telling their stories and demonstrating impact. Clearly more local African innovators need to attract these same volumes of funding. Funders also need to invest in identifying more homegrown social innovators and supporting their scaling strategies.

Implement, monitor, measure and report

Once the funding is received, it has to be deployed specifically for the purposes for which it was intended. Managing money judiciously is just as difficult as raising it in the first place.

Social innovators have to actively monitor how the money is utilized, measure impact and results and provide regular financial and impact reports to the investment or funding team. Investors often plan due diligence trips before and after their investments, and some expect board seats, depending on the size of their investments and the value that they believe that they can bring to the entity. For example, both Draper Richard Kaplan Foundation and Acumen require board seats as part of their investments into social innovations.

Impact investors also expect that the innovator will work diligently to achieve the pre-set targets to enable them effectively exit within 3–7 years, depending on the pre-negotiated terms.

Savings mechanisms

Beyond raising funds internally or externally, social innovators have to think strategically about savings mechanisms to ensure that they have funding in the future. Specific examples of strategies that are utilized by social enterprises and nonprofits in Africa include:

- Fixed deposit in cash held in banks: some banks provide double digit returns for sizeable fixed deposits in many African countries. Social innovators should actively identify such opportunities to generate some investment income from the cash held in their bank accounts.
- Endowments managed by asset management firms: social ventures which largely depend on grants benefit from setting up formal endowments. This allows the organization to set aside a pool of funds which it invests into stocks and bonds, ensuring that the invested funds and generated interest income are untouched for a defined period of time. After a predefined period, the interest income can then be utilized to cover a portion of the organization's expenses.

Ultimately, the income generated from the endowment can sustain the organization during the lean fundraising years.

• Investments: organizations can invest in fixed assets such as land and buildings, or purchase stocks and bonds for short-term investments which could ultimately appreciate and generate funds for future use.

LEAP Africa utilizes all three savings mechanisms under the supervision of a very experienced and investment savvy board of directors. It owns its office space in Lagos, established an endowment managed by one of the leading banks in Africa, and also maintains some cash in a fixed deposit. Social innovators in Africa need to become more astute about strategies for generating investment income and saving to ensure the long-term sustainability of their initiatives.

Summary

Financing the scaling of social innovations on the African continent is a difficult challenge. It requires creativity, credibility, financial discipline and determination. There are a range of options that are available to committed social innovators and their teams ranging from internally generated income options such as fee for service and cross subsidization and externally generated funds such as grants, awards, fellowships, challenge funds, crowd funding and loans.

African social innovators have to deepen their financial knowledge and expertise and become more investment ready to leverage the growing pool of funding opportunities that are available to them.

Notes

1   Cohen, Ronald, Sahlman, William 2013, 'Social impact investing will be the new venture capital', *Harvard Business Review*, January 17; https://hbr.org/2013/01/social-impact-investing-will-b/
2   Osberg Sally, Martin Roger, *Two Keys to Sustainable Social Enterprise*, *Harvard Business Review*, May 2015 Issue; https://hbr.org/2015/05/two-keys-to-sustainable-social-enterprise
3   Jahani, Mirza and West, Elizabeth 2015 'Investing in cross-subsidy for greater impact', *Stanford Social Innovation Review*, May 27; http://ssir.org/articles/entry/investing_in_cross_subsidy_for_greater_impact
4   d-light website, accessed June 10, 2015; www.dlight.com/about-us/
5   Riders for Health 2014 Annual Report.
6   AECF 2014 Impact Report, accessed November 30, 2015; www.aecfafrica.org/downloads/AECF-2014-Impact-Report.pdf
7   SIDA Innovations Against Poverty website, accessed March 2, 2015; www.sida.se/iap
8   TradeMark East Africa Challenge Fund website, accessed July 10, 2015; www.trac-fund.com/about-us.html
9   Ashoka launched its Africa program in 1990 with the election of the first fellow in Zimbabwe. Ashoka Africa expanded to West Africa in 1992 and opened its East Africa office in 2001.
10 *Accelerating Impact: Achievements, Challenges and What's Next in Building the Impact Investing Industry*, Rockefeller Foundation 2012.

11   J.P. Morgan and Global Impact Investing Network (GIIN) 2015 Eyes on the horizon: the impact investor survey.

12   Newsline, 'Social impact bonds could boost development and job creation in SA', – Graduate School of Business, University of Cape Town April 4, 2014; www.gsb. uct.ac.za/Newsrunner/Story.asp?intContentID=1681

13   Gustafsson-Wright, Emily, Gardiner, Sophie and Putcha, Vidya 2015 *The Potential and Limitations of Impact Bonds: Lessons from the First Five Years of Experience Worldwide*, Brookings, July.

14   Wangalwa Elayne, 'Kenya leads Africa's internet access and connectivity', CNBC Africa, February 12, 2015; www.cnbcafrica.com/news/east-africa/2014/09/09/kenya-leads-internet/

15   AlliedCrowds 2nd Quarter Report 2015, July 2015; http://alliedcrowds.com/assets/July-2015.pdf

16   Meaning 'working or pulling together – synergy' in Swahili.

17   GlobalGiving website; accessed November 26, 2015; www.globalgiving.org/aboutus/

18   'Riders' PPP model: innovation in pricing and capital finance', 5th International Social Innovation Research Conference, ISIRC, September 2013 Saïd Business School, University of Oxford.

19   Battilana, Julie, Lee, Matthew, Walker, John and Dorsey, Cheryl 2012 'In search of the hybrid ideal', *Stanford Social Innovation Review*, Summer 2012; http://ssir.org/articles/entry/in_search_of_the_hybrid_ideal

5 Partnerships for scaling

If you want to go fast, go alone; if you want to go far, go with others.

(African proverb)

Introduction

In the three scaling frameworks shared in Chapter 1, partnerships within and across sectors was identified as a key strategy for scaling. More specifically, in *Scaling Up: From Vision to Large-scale Change: A Management Framework for Practitioners*,[1] Larry Cooley and Richard Kohl of Management Systems International (MSI), emphasize three major pathways for scaling: expansion, replication and collaboration. All three paths have one key principle in common – partnerships – the need to work with other stakeholders in different sectors to reach more people, spread ideas, change policies and achieve high-impact social change.

On face value, forming partnerships appears logical and relatively straightforward but in practice it is often very difficult and complex. As reinforced by the Case Foundation in their publication *Fearless Principles*,

> Partnerships with new players and across sectors tend to be few and far between. Sticking with the tried and true may help us sleep better at night, but it stifles innovation and makes it hard to make the big bets necessary to move the needle on the serious problems we face. A fearless approach embraces new people and unlikely partnerships, recognizing that innovation comes from new combinations.[2]

On the African continent, building partnerships is one of the most difficult barriers to scaling. This difficulty is largely linked to significant distrust among actors, the intense competition for the perceived 'small pie' of resources and support structures and the fear of giving up control. Partnerships are also challenging in an environment where there is a high level of bureaucracy and red tape within government institutions which ordinarily should serve as catalysts for collaborations and innovations. In reality, scaling impact cannot occur without cross-sector collaborations, rooted in shared values and a desire to achieve collective impact.

This chapter outlines the steps for building partnerships across and within sectors based on the experiences of social innovators on the African continent who are scaling. This includes 1) mapping the 'ecosystem' which can and may affect the work, followed by 2) assessing the landscape and 3) developing a strategy for interfacing with all key actors. Finally, social innovators actively build partnerships based on a shared vision and values, proactively shaping their ecosystems and forming strategic cross-sector collaborations that foster scaling.

Mapping the ecosystem

Rooted in biology, the term 'ecosystem'[3] refers to complex webs of interrelated organisms, or players, each with their own roles, influencing each other in some capacity. In reality, every entity operates within an ecosystem and a first step in shaping landscapes is to identify which actors operate in it.

A useful framework for mapping the key players in the ecosystem uses the classification developed by Paul N. Bloom and J. Gregory Dees in their article titled, "Cultivate your Ecosystem" published in the *Stanford Social Innovation Review*. This framework, adapted to incorporate the key layers of complexity in African context, specifically examines the key actors by sector. The public sector includes key government agencies, parastatals and ministries at the continental, regional, federal, state or district, and local levels. The private sector includes actors operating in the formal and informal economies, micro, small, medium-sized, large, and multinational companies. Civil society includes non-governmental organizations (NGOs), faith-based organizations (FBOs), community-based organizations (CBOs), nonprofit organizations (NPOs), trade unions, industry associations, formal and informal clusters, political parties and traditional institutions. Development partners include – bi-lateral and multi-lateral agencies, trusts, local and international foundations and international NGOs. The other(s) category simply captures any stakeholder which does not fit into the previous categories.

Beyond the identification of the key actors, the mapping is incomplete unless the actors are grouped based on their relationship to the innovation or organization behind the innovation. This categorization consists of the following:

- **Direct beneficiaries** refer to the clients, beneficiaries or customers whose lives are impacted by the innovation. The indirect beneficiaries do not have first-hand contact with the innovation but their lives are still impacted through their engagement with the direct beneficiaries or a positive spill-over effect of the innovation.
- **Resource providers** refer to individuals and groups that contribute financial, human, and technology resources for the scaling of the innovation. They also share knowledge, linkages, networks, and may serve as brokers.

- **Allies and champions** refer to organizations that have a shared vision and values and are passionate about the same cause as the social innovator. They offer complementary services in the scaling process and typically perform critical steps in the social entrepreneur's theory of change.
- **Competitors** include both organizations that attempt to serve the same beneficiaries with similar services or engage with the resource providers for support for similar interventions.
- **Opponents** contribute to the problems social entrepreneurs are addressing, undermine the ability of their organizations to achieve and sustain their intended impact, or oppose their efforts politically.
- **Affected or influential bystanders** have no direct impact in the short-term, but could positively or negatively influence the scaling of the initiative or could be converted to any of the other categories above.

The table below summarizes these groupings and serves as a useful tool for social innovators who are committed to mapping the ecosystems in which they operate.

Once this mapping is completed the social innovator needs to reflect on the implications for the intervention and to feed the insights gained from this mapping into designing their strategy for cross-sector collaborators and shaping the ecosystem. For example, allies and champions are key stakeholders in advocating

Table 5.1 Ecosystem mapping framework

	Public sector	*Private sector*	*Civil society*	*Development partners*	*Other(s)*
Span	Federal, state and local, regional, continental	Formal, informal economy – micro, small, medium, large and multi-national national businesses	NGOs, NPOs, FBOs, CBOs, traditional organizations, trade unions, clusters, political parties etc.	Bi-lateral, multi-lateral agencies, local and international foundations etc.	

Categorization

Direct and indirect beneficiaries

Resource providers

Allies and champions

Competitors

Opponents

Affected or influential bystanders

Source: Adapted from the classification developed by Paul N. Bloom and J. Gregory Dees in their article titled 'Cultivate your Ecosystem' published in the *Stanford Social Innovation Review*, Winter 2008; www.ssireview.org/articles/entry/cultivate_your_ecosystem

for changes in the ecosystem and galvanizing additional support from affected or influential bystanders. Opponents and competitors need to be proactively and carefully managed to ensure that they do not undermine the scaling efforts.

Assessing the landscape

The second step required in this process of navigating the ecosystem is to assess and critically understand the landscape in which the social innovation will scale. The complexity of the landscape depends on whether the community or even country is in a phase of growth, contraction, conflict or post-conflict. There are at least three different lenses to consider when assessing the landscape of the ecosystem: political and regulatory environment, geography and infrastructure, and culture and social fabric.

Political and regulatory environment

Across Africa, the government at the regional, federal, state/district, local and community levels determines policies, controls large amounts of capital and remains the largest employer and provider of basic human services, including education and healthcare. In addition, the government determines the rules, regulations, level of bureaucracy and corruption that pervades the operating environment and affects the activities of social innovators. As a result, in the landscape assessment, social innovators have to answer a few critical questions:

Influence

- Do you operate in a local government, state, district or country, where the government wants to make positive change?
- Are there potential champions within the government? Does any group within the government oppose specific interventions or innovations?
- How much influence do the key actors either in support or against the social innovation have, and what is their scope for engagement?

Life cycle

- What is the timeframe of the intervention or scaling activity relative to the life cycle of the government?
- When will the individual and collective terms of the government officials end? How will this change affect the scaling process, both positively and negatively?

Niche or strategic entry point

- Is there a location that is representative of the needs in the region that can serve as a great testing ground and/or launching pad for scaling?
- Does this location have a favorable political landscape?

Policies and regulations

- Are there policies and regulations that govern the industry or the particular intervention that needs to be scaled?
- What is the nature of the regulation and does it support or hurt the intervention?
- Has the government put in place the right legal structures to ensure recognition and protection of property rights?
- What is the level of enforcement of the regulation, and the potential opportunities that are available to alter the regulation and potentially introduce new regulations?

Geography and infrastructure

In sub-Saharan Africa, the landscape assessment of geography and infrastructure is critical to understanding and navigating ecosystems. This is especially critical for innovations that depend on infrastructure for scaling, given the glaring disparities that still exist between urban and rural areas on the continent, with relation to electricity, telephone and internet access, feeder roads, and affordable transportation. For example, given the widespread usage of M-Pesa in Kenya and the 52.3 percent[4] internet penetration, the country has become the hub for social innovation on the continent. Indeed, innovations that leverage technology and mobile payment systems scale much faster in Kenya than they would in Ethiopia, Burundi or Sierra Leone, where internet penetration is still in the single digits.

A thorough understanding of the challenges of navigating the landscape will enable the social innovators to develop creative strategies for circumventing these challenges.

Culture and the social fabric

African ecosystems are inherently complex because of the layers of traditional, religious and cultural stakeholders that co-exist alongside the formal systems and institutions. Sometimes these informal institutions play an even more important role than the formal structures that exist. The vast diversity of languages, religions and cultures within Africa can create an additional hurdle when attempting to scale beyond regions and across borders. Rather than seeing the complexity of the diverse landscape as a challenge, a social innovator can see this as an opportunity. By taking the time and conducting the necessary research, a social innovator can gain critical insights into the way of life of the people, their norms and values, religious diversity, the role of women and youth, consideration for dominant groups, minority groups, social networks, and demographic trends, which can facilitate rather than hinder the progress of their work.

It is equally important to assess the power dynamics that exist in the society, especially as they relate to women, children, the elderly, people with special needs, and minority groups. Indeed, understanding how to address the needs of these groups is critical to ensuring that they are not marginalized or neglected during the scaling process.

In any operating environment, one must also understand the 'gatekeepers' and the roles they play in allowing access and supporting or preventing change in their communities. More specifically, social innovators need to understand the roles that religious and traditional rulers play in some communities, which are often regarded as more important than the formal government structures. Indeed, partnerships with these key influencers are a critical prerequisite for changing mindsets or introducing new initiatives in communities.

This assessment of the political and regulatory environment, the geography and infrastructure and the culture and social fabric is pivotal to determining how to navigate the ecosystem. It reveals which partnerships are critical for scaling a social innovation and how to engage with all key stakeholders in order to achieve results. Indeed, a thorough mapping and assessment of the landscape informs the strategy for shaping the ecosystem and enhances the social innovator's likelihood of success.

BOX 5.1: KEY QUESTIONS FOR INNOVATORS

How much do you understand and influence your operating landscape?

Political and regulatory environment

1   **Regulatory environment**
    - What are the current local, national or regional regulations that hinder or help the scaling of the social innovation?
    - What regulations should be introduced or modified to foster the scaling process?

2   **Political influence**
    - Are there any potential champions within the government at the local, state and federal levels?
    - Does any group within the government oppose specific interventions or innovations?
    - What influence can your organization exert to positively influence the key actors either in support or against the social innovation?
    - How will the life cycle of the government (i.e. when the individual and collective terms of the government officials end) affect the scaling process, both positively and negatively? How can your team mitigate the potentially negative impact?

Niche or strategic entry point

- Is there a location that is representative of the needs in the region that can serve as a suitable testing ground and/or launching pad for scaling?
    - Does this location have a favourable political landscape?

Infrastructure

- What key infrastructure is critical for the scaling of your innovation?
- What is the state of this critical infrastructure in your context and how can your team address or navigate the deficits to enable scaling?
    - Consider each of the following essential services:
        - power (grid and off grid solutions)
        - telephone, cellular communications and internet access
        - feeder roads
        - affordable transportation
        - water
        - financial services
        - others.

Culture and social fabric

- Outside of the political sphere, who are the key influencers in the communities in which you operate?
- What are their key levers of influence?
- How can you work with them to support your scaling efforts?
    - What are the power dynamics in society and how can these be positively influenced especially as they relate to:
        - women and girls?
        - the elderly?
        - people with special needs?
        - religious and ethnic minority groups?
        - other vulnerable groups?

Shaping the ecosystem

Three steps are required for shaping the ecosystem – the social innovator builds a constituency, forms strategic partnerships and engages in a step-by-step and systematic process in order to achieve sustainable impact at scale.

Build a strong constituency

Social innovators who are able to scale their initiatives invest in building a strong constituency of supporters. This typically includes their direct and indirect beneficiaries, allies and champions, which would have already been identified through the mapping process. In some cases, these groups could be recognized as a critical mass of people which could mobilize the support required to reach a tipping point. However, in many cases, especially where the regulation may be at odds with the social innovation's interventions or where there is significant resistance from the public sector, the innovator has to explore other avenues. They could partner with competitors and attract individuals to join the constituency in order to strengthen their collective voices and ensure sustainable and scalable growth and development.

A prerequisite to building a strong constituency is credibility and legitimacy. Social innovators who have both can persuade relevant decision makers, resource providers and opinion leaders that new solutions are necessary and desirable. They can also determine exactly which arguments, appeals, or advocacy strategies are likely to persuade the decision makers to adopt new policies or change their existing policies to support the scaling effort.

There are three key steps to building legitimacy and credibility:

1   Develop a strong brand name

Creative social entrepreneurs engage credible spokespeople and celebrities to serve as advocates. These individuals already have strong constituencies and can engage them to generate support and enhance the credibility of a social innovation. In addition, the use of images, slogans and symbols, shared through a robust advertising and marketing strategy which leverages both traditional and digital media strengthens the brand name. Utilizing social media, including Twitter, Facebook and Instagram and releasing periodic articles via a blog or other influential sites cultivates a critical following online, which is important for most social change efforts.

2   Ensure strong internal governance structures

This includes instituting a credible board of directors, composed of individuals who are respected for their track record of success and commitment to integrity. In addition, as an innovation scales through expansion and collaboration, some social innovators in Africa have established advisory committees composed of respected individuals from the local community in which the innovation is being scaled, to enhance the credibility of the initiative and increase community ownership. This advisory committee does not operate as a formal board of directors, but meets periodically to provide guidance and support for the local implementation process.

3   Demonstrate and report impact

Legitimacy and credibility are enhanced through transparent key performance indicators, with further endorsement by independent credible audit and/or performance monitoring groups. In addition, innovators actively publish their impact in their annual reports, on their websites and also engage the media as an effective vehicle for showcasing their impact within communities, countries and regions. Ultimately, the impact of the innovation and the ability to utilize media and creative communication strategies, including community engagement, to amplify this impact is critical to developing and sustaining credibility and legitimacy.

As aptly described by the January 2013 UNDP Guidance Note, *Scaling Up Development Programmes*, the often long and drawn out process of building legitimacy has been described as,

> going slow to go fast. In the case of policy change, legitimizing change is essential for getting policies approved, budgetary priorities adopted, and developing the broader and deeper base of support needed for implementation by bureaucratic institutions and others. More generally, it is critical for attracting potential adopting organizations; for persuading funders to provide support; and for ensuring a warm reception of the model among new locations, client populations, and potentially competing organizations.

For extremely difficult changes which could affect the masses of people, social innovators work diligently to build broad-based awareness and local ownership. This could involve organizing grassroots campaigns, implementing public education programs, organizing and conducting policy debates, and advocacy campaigns with the political parties, legislators and legislative committees. It could also require direct outreach to specific interest groups including traditional rulers, business groups, faith-based communities, organized labor and other civil society groups.

Forming strategic partnerships across sectors

While there is a range of potential stakeholders to engage with, most social entrepreneurs who scale in Africa partner with actors in the public, private, social or development sectors. The nature of these partnerships is diverse as outlined below:

Partnering with the public sector

Governments have a critical role to play in supporting the scaling of social innovations. They can provide financial and in-kind support for defraying fixed costs for proven business models. In addition, they can incorporate the innovation into their service delivery models – especially for sectors such as health and education where they serve as the primary provider. They can also provide an enabling environment for the social innovation to scale, including introducing appropriate policies and regulations. Similarly, they can use their convening power to attract actors in an ecosystem and encourage them to partner to scale social innovations.

However, despite the numerous potential roles that governments can play in scaling, social innovators often struggle with engaging them in the process of shaping ecosystems in Africa. Interviews conducted as field research for this book suggest that there are typically three approaches utilized by social entrepreneurs in Africa. These strategies include:

Alignment with the government

Innovators work closely with governments to pilot and scale their initiatives, often depending on the government for cash and in-kind support and legitimacy. They are often viewed as implementers of government initiatives. If the government is stable and credible, all parties are happy and they are branded as insiders. However, their initiatives and interventions could be totally sidelined and even destroyed if the government changes. Too often, the social entrepreneurs are punished by the incoming administration for their strong alliances with the previous government.

> **Example: Riders for Health** completely aligns with the government to provide healthcare services to last-mile customers. It manages and maintains fleets of vehicles for health-focused partners, predominantly Ministries of Health in sub-Saharan Africa. Fifty percent of its costs are covered from contractual relationships with Ministries of Health.

Circumvention of government

These entrepreneurs avoid governments and have no links or connections with them beyond paying taxes and abiding by the laws of the land. Operating and attempting to scale under this ideology works in some contexts, either where the government is not required for scaling and the regulatory environment is supportive or where the government is obstructive and repressive. Ultimately, this approach is often not sustainable, especially with increased budgetary and local and national growth. When the governments start to take notice, they may become threatened and antagonistic, simply because they do not understand the genesis and history of the social innovations.

Organizations focused on environmental protection, pro-democracy, anti-corruption, human rights – including the rights of women and special interest groups (including prochoice and the LGBT community) often deliberately circumvent the government in many African countries, given the prevailing policies.

Cooperation with government

These entrepreneurs develop creative ways to partner with the government, but do not completely align with them. They work diligently to maintain ties with the government, and engage them in an advisory capacity, but are not dependent on them. They also leverage the extensive reach of the government's infrastructure and public service networks to deploy their social innovations, but this is done without absolute dependence on the government's resources. They give the government credit for their modest successes, but stay relatively politically neutral. Their focus is on building credibility and mutual trust, scaling what works and providing a learning agenda.

> **Example: CLEEN Foundation** was established in 1998 in Nigeria to promote public safety, security and accessible justice by changing the attitudes of the Nigerian police towards the public and by educating average Nigerians about their rights and the legal system. Faced with stiff resistance from both sides of the divide from the onset, the organization chose to build bridges. According to CLEEN's founder, Mr. Innocent Chukwuma, in conversation for this book.
>
>> We knew that we had to pursue a different tack from the previous approach utilized by the Nigerian human rights groups which consisted primarily of accusations, newspaper campaigns, and court cases. As a result, we came in offering partnership and empathy, ensuring that community priorities would be infused in policing and working to move the police away from regime policing philosophy to democratic policing.
>
> Early in its history, CLEEN worked with the Nigerian Police Force to revive and strengthen its internal accountability mechanisms such as the Police Public Complaints Bureau (PCB) in six Nigerian states. It encouraged the police to make these processes open and transparent to members of the public. These efforts exposed the gross misconduct of many police officers, leading to the dismissal of over 5,000!
>
> CLEEN also conducted a survey on the root causes of police–community violence in Nigeria, which led to the publication of the book *Police–Community Violence in Nigeria* (Alemika and Chukwuma 2000). The study revealed that there was limited interaction between the police and the communities they served in Nigeria, outside law enforcement, which in turn fostered hostilities. In direct response to these findings, CLEEN piloted the establishment of community policing forums in 14 local government areas in Nigeria between 2001 and 2003. These efforts proved extremely effective, not only in building bridges between the police and community residents, but also in contributing significantly towards the reporting, investigation, and reduction in the incidence of crime. According to Mrs. Fatia Sani, the President of the Market Women Association in Abuja, 'Crime in Zone 7 is now a thing of the past! CLEEN has brought us closer to the police, which an average market woman used to fear. Before we thought the police were our enemies. Now, we know that the police are our friends'.
>
> For Jacaranda, it recognized early in its history that the government provided 90 percent of the maternity services in Kenya. Driven by a desire to transform the landscape, it shifted its operating model from a provider of high

quality maternity care via clinics to a trainer and provider of advisory services to government facilities. Jacaranda's two maternity hospitals currently serve as centres of excellence. In its roll-out phase, it is focused on selectively partnering with counties that are early adopters, who share its values and can work collaboratively to show what works. According to Nick Pearson, the founder of Jacaranda, interviewed for this book, 'In healthcare, you cannot survive without partnerships – with the government, private sector and civil society.'

Ultimately, the theory of change of an organization, its business model, the sector in which it operates, and its vision for scaling will largely determine which government engagement approach is most suitable. Typically, players engaged in service provision in the health and education sectors have to align or cooperate with the government because of its dominant role as a regulator and primary provider in these sectors.

Partnering with other key actors

Beyond the government, social innovators also partner with other actors including the private sector, civil society, and the development community. For example, the private sector can leverage its deep funding base to provide financing for scale through investments, loans, or grants. It can also utilize its supply chain and distribution networks to accelerate widespread distribution and its media presence, public relations, and communication resources to promote increased awareness. In addition, it can capitalize upon its technological expertise to provide more effective ways to deploy solutions. Similarly, civil society can use its stronger links with and legitimacy at the grassroots, its lower costs structure, and its ability to galvanize volunteers to scale innovations. Development partners can leverage their global networks for knowledge sharing and their funding to scale initiatives, build capacity and invest in measurement and evaluation.

Even though strategic partnerships are still relatively novel across Africa, there is a growing recognition of their importance and increased interest from social innovators to actively foster and structure strategic partnerships across sectors.

BOX 5.2: KEY QUESTIONS FOR INNOVATORS

Are you poised to shape your ecosystem via partnerships?

- Do you have a strong constituency?
  - Who are the key stakeholders represented in this constituency?
  - What can your organization do to build a stronger constituency?
- What can your organization do to strengthen its credibility and legitimacy? Can it establish?

- a strong brand name?
- an internal governance structure?
- a transparent set of performance indicators?
- a system for sharing performance results with key stakeholders?
- What is the nature of your relationship with the:
  - local, state and federal government (e.g. do you align, circumvent or cooperate with the government)? How does this relationship help or hurt your scaling process with the:
  - private sector? How does this relationship help or hurt your scaling process? What steps can you take to change this?
  - nonprofit sector? How does this relationship help or hurt your scaling process? What steps can you take to change this?
  - development community? How does this relationship help or hurt your scaling process? What steps can you take to change this?
  - other actors?

Critical prerequisites for successful partnerships

Popular management theory suggests that successful partnerships are hinged on trust and mutual respect. However, in the African social sector, though important, these are not typically the most critical success factors that social innovators need to consider prior to formalizing a partnership with another key organization in the ecosystem. Instead, social innovators should prioritize the following five prerequisites.

A shared vision of solutions to the social problem and a collective commitment to working collaboratively to implement them. This includes political will on the part of the government where it is a critical stakeholder in the scaling process. It is important to recognize that social innovators and their organizations may not often share the same values with other key collaborators; however, a shared vision aligns interests and enables the stakeholders to push towards impact.

A clear understanding of what role each partner is playing to enable scaling is critical. Typically this is captured in a **partnership agreement** or a memorandum of collaboration and a decentralized managerial model with clear funding structures. This formalized document should include:

- The goals and objectives of the partnership.
- The roles and responsibilities of each stakeholder.
- The terms of use of the name and logo of each stakeholder and exactly how the partnership arrangement will be described in the public domain.
- Cost and resource sharing arrangements, where applicable.
- The time frame for the partnership – with clear start and end dates.
- Conditions which could lead to the termination of the partnership and the process for the termination.

- A commitment to making the partnership work, which requires humility, the willingness to compromise, and ability to tolerate a diversity of values, culture and approaches, provided these do not distract all parties from achieving the shared vision.
- Measurement and evaluation tools for gauging the impact of the partnership and key timelines and milestones.
- Systems and structures that enable regular communications – including formal meetings and reports to share information, provide updates on progress and lessons from failures and agreement on next steps.

Case studies on the power of cross sector collaborations

Consider four key examples of actors scaling via partnerships from different angles: 1) nonprofit-led, Action Health Incorporated, 2) donor-led ESSPIN, 3) public-sector led Ethiopian Community Exchange and 4) an international social-franchise model Aflatoun broadening its reach to Nigeria in partnership with LYNX.

Nonprofit led social innovation

Focused initially on reaching hundreds of young people through school clubs and after school activities, between 1996 and 2002, Action Health Incorporated (AHI) engaged in the difficult quest to incorporate sexuality education into the core curriculum of public schools across Nigeria. An interview with Mrs. Nike Esiet, the co-founder of Action Health revealed:

> prior to 1989, there was a culture of silence around young people's sexuality in Nigeria. AHI contributed to moving Nigeria from a point of denial and apathy about the poor status of young people's sexual health indices to a context where universal access to sexuality education for young people is now on the national education policy agenda.

In order to achieve this seemingly impossible feat, AHI utilized a multi-pronged strategy, which included:

Developing a clear message and a sense of urgency

Riding on the glaring statistics of early sexual encounters, prevalence of HIV/AIDs and unwanted pregnancy, AHI created a sense of urgency about the need to teach young people about their bodies. It identified the government as the critical partner for scaling and engaged in targeted advocacy to raise awareness and engage them as the lead partner.

Creating alliances with civil society organisations and government agencies

From the onset, AHI recognized that partnerships would be critical to its success. In 1996, it convened a task force that mobilized over 100 organisations, ranging from youth-serving agencies to religious associations, to reach consensus in endorsing a set of national sexuality education guidelines. AHI then used this document in 1999, in collaboration with the Federal Ministry of Education, to secure government's approval of the policy for universal access to sexuality education. It then partnered with the Federal Ministry of Health to develop the Framework for Addressing Adolescent Reproductive Health. It also facilitated the development of the National Family Life and HIV Education (FLHE) Curriculum in collaboration with the Federal Ministry of Education and the Nigerian Educational Research and Development Council.

Conducting extensive research and creating resource materials

AHI developed 38 publications and a curriculum, including the *AHI Comprehensive Sexuality Education Trainers' Resource Manual, Can We Really Talk About It? A Self-Help Guide For Talking With Your Adolescents, A Guide To Setting Up Health And Life Planning Clubs* and *Youth Making A Difference (Anti-AIDS Club)*. It also published the *Family Life and HIV Education Students' Handbook* and *Teachers Guide* to facilitate learning and effective classroom delivery of FLHE to junior secondary school students across Nigeria. These publications were not only extremely user-friendly, but filled an important gap in the country, because they were designed specifically for educators and youth and addressed the unique needs of each audience in the Nigerian context.

Engaging credible and distinct stakeholders to play distinct roles in the scaling up effort

AHI recognized that it could not work in isolation and needed the support of a range of actors to scale. It identified and engaged a range of stakeholders who played key roles including 1) youth and reproductive health nongovernmental organisations who provided teacher in-service training on the FLHE curriculum and ongoing support to schools; 2) secondary schools who were responsible for classroom teaching and extracurricular activities; and 3) teacher-training institutes who delivered the student teacher training. 4) development partners and foundations such as the MacArthur and Ford Foundations which provided financial and in-kind support to enable the scaling effort. In addition, AHI continued to play an oversight role, ensuring quality, measurement and evaluation and building capacity.

Showcasing the impact of its work in Lagos State

It created a model which other states could replicate, and which ultimately could be rolled out at a national level. Given AHI's long partnership with Lagos State, it was able to work alongside the state to implement the curriculum and to demonstrate tangible results. This rapid success set Lagos apart and positioned it as a model for others. Dr. Olakunle Lawal, former Commissioner for Education in Lagos State said in interview for this book,

> Full implementation of the FLHE programme in all our 311 public junior secondary schools has been possible because of the technical support provided by AHI. This accomplishment generated so much interest among our counterparts in other states and delegations from no less than eight other state ministries of education have come to understudy the work on FLHE in Lagos.

Countering dissenting voices and the backlash in the mass media

Conservatives consistently propagated the erroneous notion that access to sexuality education would encourage adolescents to become more sexually active. Given that sexuality education was largely perceived as incompatible with prevailing traditional and religious values and norms in Nigeria, AHI faced immense pressure from groups who strongly opposed sexuality education as not being in the best interest of adolescents. Through a concerted effort, AHI effectively converted these dissenting voices through evidenced-based advocacy, public education and community mobilization into advocates and champions. It also actively engaged parent–teacher associations, community leaders and the media. For example, the strongest opposition to the scaling effort in Lagos State came from the Catholic mothers. AHI actively established a strong relationship with the Permanent Secretary of the Ministry of Education who was a Catholic woman and she became a champion for the scaling effort, eventually swaying the Catholic mothers.

Investing in sustainability

Beyond the policy, AHI recognized that the state governments would need to invest in sustaining the delivery of high-quality curriculum and instruction to ensure impact. To this end, Dr. Uwem Esiet, the other co-founder of AHI Inc. said in interview,

> we started with the end in mind, doing everything from the beginning to ensure that our partner would believe in our intent, understand it, and catch the vision. We remained in their engine room and got them to take the leadership so that when we pull out, they can continue.

The 2009–2011 National FLHE Curriculum Implementation Scorecard which measured government funding, state support, resource material, school preparedness, teacher training and state level monitoring and evaluation, revealed that all states were still implementing the curriculum, six states were achieving high-impact results, with Lagos far ahead.

Action Health Incorporated's experience is most instructive because it is one of the rare examples of a social innovation that has scaled via cross-sector collaborations in Africa.

Donor-led social innovation

Funded by the UK Department for International Development (DFID) and managed by a consortium of partners led by Cambridge Education, the Education Sector Support Programme in Nigeria (ESSPIN) was introduced in 2008 to improve learning outcomes for primary school children. It is focused on six Nigerian states – Enugu, Jigawa, Kaduna, Kano, Kwara and Lagos. From 2008 to 2014, the team received £92m (approximately $140m), and the intervention has been extended until January 2017 on an additional budget of £33m (approximately $50m).

The ESSPIN team followed a step-by-step engagement process which mirrors the partnership framework outlined earlier including mapping key stakeholders, building legitimacy and credibility and designing, piloting and eventually scaling sustainably.

Building legitimacy: measurement and evaluation (M & E) and advocacy

The ESSPIN team conducted five baseline studies in 2010[5] – a teacher development needs assessment, a head teacher survey, a classroom observation study, a monitoring of learning achievement study, and a community perception survey – to inform the intervention process. The results of these studies were alarming. The teacher development needs assessment revealed that most teachers across the six states had inadequate knowledge and competency levels to teach the primary school curriculum. Over 90 percent of teachers scored under 30 percent on tests based on Grade 4 mathematics and English language curricula. This assessment indicated that teachers would be unable to lead school-based professional development activities to raise standards. In addition, the head teacher survey revealed that nearly two-thirds of a head teacher's time was spent on activities unconnected to leading or managing a school, with little evidence of development planning and efforts at school improvement. The community survey demonstrated that school-based management committees were largely inactive and in one state, only 1 percent of parents had attended one meeting during an entire school year. These baseline research findings informed the design of the interventions, the measurement and evaluation framework and equipped ESSPIN with hard data for engaging and challenging state governments to embrace change.

Mapping key stakeholders

The team engaged in a comprehensive mapping exercise which identified the specific stakeholders to own and drive implementation of the reform programme. This included state-specific agencies, traditional and religious leaders, parent groups, community-based organisations and the private sector. This process revealed that the State Universal Basic Education Board (SUBEB), which has the direct mandate to manage basic education would serve as the key champion in each state. Ministries of education were also engaged on the basis of their oversight role and responsibility for governance functions including data management, strategic planning and budgeting, policy regulations and quality assurance services. In addition, specific individuals in each community were identified to serve as members of the school-based management committee, charged with galvanizing community and private sector support for the schools and holding the school leadership accountable for results.

Designing, piloting, scaling

The baseline results and the mapping of key stakeholders informed the design of a multi-pronged program, rooted in three levels of government (federal, state and local) and adopted an integrated reform program focused on improving school performance. From a pilot, the program was scaled, 'to provide and support the use of structured training materials for teachers, work with head teachers to improve academic leadership and school improvement planning, and involve communities through the establishment of well-functioning school-based management committees (SBMCs).'[6] Specific interventions included training for head teachers to improve their leadership effectiveness, training teachers to improve their competency and personal effectiveness and building the capacity of personnel from civil society organizations to improve their advocacy and community engagement skills.

At the end of 2014, ESSPIN's school level programmes had reached over 10,000 schools in the six Nigerian states, with over 3.7 million children enrolled in schools that have received ESSPIN support. Researchers from Oxford Policy Management revealed that across most of the key levels of support, head teachers, teachers and students in ESSPIN schools outperformed their peers.

Sustainability

ESSPIN's theory of change is hinged on the notion that evidence of impact from the pilot schools, proving that the school improvement program (SIP) approach works, would convince state governments to invest their own resources in scale up. To this end, the ESSPIN team actively engaged in a broad-based advocacy effort to persuade state governments to channel more resources towards expanding the benefits of SIP to a greater number of schools. It also instituted a quarterly meeting of Education Commissioners from the six states to review their progress, share experiences and, ultimately, take responsibility for funding the required expansion. As of September 2015, only three of the six states (Kano, Jigawa and Lagos) have managed to fund aspects of SIP expansion from their annual state budgets. The rest have relied on the federal government and the Partnership on Education for funding.

Government-led social innovation

Prior to the establishment of the Ethiopia Commodity Exchange (ECX)

Ethiopian agricultural markets had been characterized by high costs and risks of transacting, with only one third of output reaching the market. Commodity buyers and sellers tended to trade only with those they knew, to avoid the risk of being cheated or default, because there was no assurance of product quality or quantity.

In this context, small-scale farmers, who produce 95 percent of Ethiopia's agricultural output, had inaccurate information about market prices, low bargaining power, and did not engage in product grading. At the mercy of merchants in the nearest and only market they knew, and unable to negotiate better prices or access facilities to store the surplus of their production, farmers often lost motivation to increase production. This resulted in volatile prices and food scarcity during some periods of the year, and high consumer prices.

Overview of ECX

The Ethiopia Commodity Exchange (ECX), was initiated in 2008 as a marketplace or platform that facilitates agricultural produce trade between buyers and sellers, and protects both farmers and traders from price drops and price hikes, respectively. ECX harnesses innovation, technology, and storage infrastructures to mobilize products from smallholder farmers and ensure product quality, delivery and payment. ECX provides transparent price information for both farmers and buyers, and currently focuses on a few products, such as coffee, sesame, haricot beans, maize and wheat.

Key scaling challenges

At its early stages, the Ethiopia Commodity Exchange faced a number of challenges, including limited capacity in terms of skills and telecommunications infrastructure; refusal of traditional brokers to accept the new system; limitations in the provision of facilities, especially internet services; disruption of power supply that affected service delivery to customers; and conflicts due to poor contractual agreement among suppliers and transporters.[7]

Impact

Despite early challenges, ECX has grown from trading 138,000 tons of produce and 100 members in 2008/09, to 2.5 million tons of traded commodities in July 2014, worth 96.7 billion Birr (US$4.7 billion), and 346 members. It has 14,725 clients, and 10 percent farmer cooperative unions reaching out to 2.7 million small farmers (ECX Record Performance, 2014).

Transformative scale

The dynamic Ethiopian Commodity Exchange is further spreading its information feed. Now customers can access general information and their accounts through SMS and voice telephone ('interactive voice receiver') systems.[8]

Other African countries such as Ghana and Nigeria are engaged in establishing similar platforms and have participated in study tours and consultations with the ECX.

International social franchising

Aflatoun (Child Savings International) is a nongovernmental organization which was registered in the Netherlands in 2005 with the objective of unleashing the potential of children through social and financial education.

Background

Jeroo Billimoria started the concept in Mumbai in 1991 after she visited shelters for street children. She found that although the children were quite entrepreneurial and had a high earning potential, they were destined to a life of poverty as they spent their earnings recklessly because they did not believe they had a future. Under the guidance of the Tata Institute, Billimoria set up Meljol (which means 'coming together' in Hindi), a programme that featured the core elements of what is now known as Aflatoun. It used games, art, stories and play to teach children about saving money.

The program made a tangible difference in the lives of children. A study conducted by Meljol revealed that 78 percent of children who participated in the programme in 2000 were still in the habit of saving money, six years later.[9] Billimoria and her colleagues decided to extend the model to other countries.

Extending the program worldwide

Aflatoun is built through partnerships with stakeholders from various sectors. The stakeholders include local community service organisations, international nongovernment organisations, microfinance institutions, banking institutions, financial regulators, ministries of education and ministries of finance. Aflatoun also collaborates with regional and sub-regional bodies and has worked closely with the East African community to harmonise financial education delivery in five partner states.

The Secretariat in the Netherlands recruits partner organizations globally based on very explicit criteria, including a shared commitment to empowering young children financially and socially.

Today, the Aflatoun Network is a dynamic, bottom-up network of interlinked partner organisations. It has 181 partners in 113 countries and reaches 3.9 million children and youth annually. The network incorporates 53,091 schools and non-formal education centres and 112,545 teachers, facilitators and peer educators. In 2014, there were 729,842 active children who saved 2.76 million euros.[10]

In order to preserve the vision of a partner-led movement, both the secretariat and the partner organisations are required to commit to their respective roles. The secretariat is committed to enabling communications across the network and amongst partners, and providing opportunities and structures for the partners to contribute their experience and expertise to add value to the program.

Aflatoun does not provide funding or top-down control to partners, due to its limited resources and its belief that each organisation should take full ownership of the program. Its partners generate funding for the program in various ways; some organisations draw on internal budget resources, while others rely on grants and local fundraising.

The program

Aflatoun and its partners cater to children in both classrooms and non-formal settings. The partners start by determining the needs of children locally and then tailoring the international materials to local content. The secretariat manages a cadre of 220 regional master trainers who provide training on behalf of Aflatoun. It also conducts regional and international learning opportunities and events and offers a comprehensive package of technical assistance that it provides to partner via the regional programme managers.

Aflatoun partnership in Nigeria – LYNX

Since 2006, Aflatoun has partnered with Linking the Youth of Nigeria through Exchange (LYNX), a local nonprofit founded by Nanre Nafzinger-Mayegun.

After a successful pilot in Lagos and Kaduna states between 2006 and 2008, LYNX started to scale up between 2008 and 2012 through partnerships. It partnered with JP Morgan, Bayelsa State Government Child Development Account (CDA) Programme and ECOMM Foundation to reach over 13,312 students in 166 schools.

LYNX continued to search for support and introduced the concept to different governmental, non-governmental and private sector organisations. The concept of child social and financial education (CSFE) became established; the United Nations Children's Fund (UNICEF) and SOS Children's Villages adopted it. Eventually at a curriculum planning meeting to incorporate CSFE into a UNICEF programme for out-of-school girls, the National Agency for Mass Literacy, Adult and Non-Formal Education (NMEC) showed interest and as a result, social and financial literacy is being incorporated into the core curriculum of NMEC, which includes its curriculum for out-of-school boys and girls and its general business studies curriculum. Through this, the CSFE will reach over 3 million children and youth in NMEC programmes in all 36 states of Nigeria.

Another opportunity to scale emerged when the Central Bank of Nigeria (CBN) launched its Financial Inclusion Policy in 2011 at the general regional meeting of Child and Youth Finance International, another LYNX partner. In 2013, the executive director of LYNX was invited to serve on the Curriculum Development Working Group (CDWG) – part of the Financial Inclusion Working Group headed by CBN.

The CDWG is collaborating with the National Educational Research and Development Council (NERDC) to incorporate financial literacy into the school curriculum for Nigerian students by the end of 2016. Some of the core concepts developed by LYNX are already being adopted by the CDWG, which will become part of the regular curriculum reaching millions of school children in the country. LYNX is currently working with banks and other financial institutions to incorporate CSFE into their products and to invest in their financial inclusion initiatives for low-income youth.

The four examples outlined above reinforce the benefits of cross-sector collaborations in propelling social innovations, enabling scaling and achieving impact. AHI's successful partnership with Lagos State and the Federal Ministry of Education, and supportive funders enabled the scaling of sexuality education across Nigeria, and stemmed the spread of HIV/AIDs and teenage pregnancies. ESSPIN's partnership with CBOs, state governments and nonprofits has transformed the educational experiences of thousands of children, improving their outcomes and future prospects. Similarly, Ethiopia Commodity Exchange and its partnership with farmers, funders, and key actors in the private sector has enhanced transparency in the commodities markets and enabled farmers to benefit from more direct links to the customers, improving their livelihoods. Finally, Aflatoun's scaling approach through social franchising and its partnership with LYNX, which in turn has partnered with a range of private, public and nonprofit actors in Nigeria, has led to financial literacy and inclusion of Nigerian youth and shaped policy for the broader industry.

Summary

Social innovations cannot scale without partnerships within and across sectors with other stakeholders. The innovator's ability to map the ecosystem, complete an assessment of the landscape and develop a strategy for interfacing with all key actors in order to inform the formation of strategic cross-sector collaborations, will ultimately determine the pace of the scaling effort.

Social innovators that are committed to forming strategic partnerships across sectors have to build legitimacy and credibility from the outset, hinged on strong governance structures, performance measurement, and a solid communications strategy. They also have to focus on achieving a shared vision for the solution to the problem and outcomes as the basis for the partnership, sometimes compromising for the greater cause.

Notes

1   Cooley, Larry and Kohl, Richard 2006 *Scaling Up – From Vision to Large-scale Change: A Management Framework for Practitioners*, Management Systems International, Washington, DC.
2   Case Foundation 2012 *The Fearless Principles*, page 18.
3   Bloom, Paul N. and Dees, J. Gregory, 2008 'Cultivate your ecosystem', *Stanford Social Innovation Review*, Winter 2008; www.ssireview.org/articles/entry/cultivate_your_ ecosystem.
4   Wangalwa, Elayne 2015 'Kenya leads Africa's internet access and connectivity', CNBC Africa, February 12; www.cnbcafrica.com/news/east-africa/2014/09/09/kenya-leads-internet/
5   Sanni, Kayode 2015 *Taking School Improvement to Scale: The Education Sector Support Programme in Nigeria* March, Cambridge Education.
6   *Scaling up School Improvement in Nigeria: Findings from a New Survey*, Oxford Policy Management, September 2015.
7   An assessment of the opportunities and challenges of the Ethiopian Commodity Exchange www.jsd-africa.com/Jsda/V13No1_Spring2011_A/PDF/An%20Assessment %20of%20the%20Opportunities%20and%20Challenges%20of%20the%20Ethiopian %20Commodity%20Exchange%20(Paul).pdf
8   Minney, Tom 2015 'Ethiopian Commodity Exchange gets online trading platform', October 13; www.africancapitalmarketsnews.com/2882/ethiopian-commodityexchange-gets-online-trading-platform/#sthash.I0GtPb8I.dpuf
9   Amar, Sush and Munk, Simon 2014 'Franchising a "fireball"', *Stanford Social Innovation Review*, Summer 2014.
10 Aflatoun website, accessed October 14, 2015; www.aflatoun.org/story/story-selected/ results-to-date

6 Supporting scaling

The roles of key stakeholders

Introduction

M-Pesa[1] is widely celebrated as one of the most successful global social innovations in the past decade. The concept for M-Pesa traces its roots to the DFID funded researchers at Gamos and the Commonwealth Telecommunications Organization. In 2002, the researchers revealed that people in various African countries were transferring airtime to their relatives or friends who were then using or reselling it. The researchers approached Safaricom in Kenya (a subsidiary of Vodafone) to explore the opportunity to create a service that would leverage the network of Safaricom airtime resellers to enable microfinance borrowers to receive and repay their loans. With funding from DFID, Safaricom launched a pilot in 2005 to test the potential for this innovation. The insights gained from the pilot, including the demand for a mobile-money transfer system, led Safaricom to launch a new mobile phone-based payment and money transfer service, called M-Pesa, with M for mobile and *Pesa* which is the Swahili word for money.

By 2015, M-Pesa had reached 19.6 million people – over 70 percent of households in Kenya and over 50 percent of the poor, unbanked and rural populations. It has also evolved from a money-transfer system to one that facilitates payments for all types of products and services – including healthcare, education, energy (especially off-grid solutions), savings, loans and investments. It spurred the emergence of numerous start-ups in Kenya, who ride on the success of the M-Pesa technology. This has also enabled Kenya to serve as the testing ground for innovations that meet the needs of low-income populations in urban and rural areas, as demonstrated by many of the case studies examined in this book. In addition, M-Pesa has been replicated and adapted in a wide range of countries, including Tanzania, South Africa, Afghanistan and India.

The M-Pesa story reinforces four important realities about scaling social innovation in Africa which have already been explored in the preceding chapters:

1 **The innovation has to fill a gap, address a need or solve a problem**. In the case of M-Pesa, there was a latent need for the unbanked and rural populations to send and receive money without bearing the high cost of transporting this money to family and friends via long distances.

2 **The right partners have to be involved.** DFID committed significant amounts of funding to the research and pilot phases, and this allowed for experimentation. In addition, DFID could have chosen to fund a pilot with a nonprofit entity in Kenya, or even brought in a large UK-based consulting firm to run the project for a few years, as is the case with many development-partner led interventions; However, in this case, DFID identified Safaricom, a dominant private sector company with large operations across Kenya. This approach proved to be the best one – not only because Safaricom had aligned interests and support systems for the pilot, but also because it had a long-term commitment to Kenya.

3 **The intervention should leverage existing infrastructure to reduce costs and enhance scaling.** Safaricom already had a large network of airtime resellers who could be leveraged to test out the model. In the event that this network was non-existent, Safaricom would have had to find a proxy or work to develop a network. It is important to note that in 2015, there are over 40,000 dedicated M-Pesa agents in Kenya. Since then the exclusivity requirement has been eased.

4 **There has to be an enabling policy environment or the opportunity to shape one.** There was no policy governing mobile money when M-Pesa was introduced. The Kenyan government, instead of cranking down on the 'unknown', provided a supportive policy and regulatory environment for M-Pesa, allowing the scheme to proceed on an experimental basis, without formal approval. This ultimately enabled the key stakeholders to shape the emergence of the current policies.

While the M-Pesa example is instructive, it is not widely representative of the history of social innovations on the African continent. The uniqueness of this example lies in the fact that DFID committed significant amounts of funding to the research and pilot phases, and the Kenyan government provided a supportive policy and regulatory environment. Sadly, most social innovators do not have the luxury of dedicated funding to conduct research on their ideas and to test their concepts through a meaningful pilot. Many African governments actively introduce policies and regulations that hinder as opposed to help the scaling of social innovations.

Africa desperately needs more M-Pesas, and this can only be accomplished when all key stakeholders commit to support scaling. This chapter explores the roles that governments, the development community, academia, the private sector and social innovators must play to support the scaling of high-impact social innovations on the continent.

Governments

The primary responsibility of governments is to create an enabling environment for social entrepreneurs to establish and scale innovations that will transform communities and countries. They are expected to reduce the hurdles associated with registering entities, obtaining patents and trademarks, and ensuring property rights protection. In addition, they are expected to minimize corruption and red tape associated with normal operations and to encourage the private sector and citizens to invest in social innovators and provide financial and in-kind donations to the social sector. This can be achieved by creating tax incentives for individuals and private companies that support social enterprises, as is the case in the United States and the United Kingdom, where such donations are tax deductible.

Beyond creating an enabling environment, governments should actively support social entrepreneurs who need to be assured that governments at the local, district, federal, and regional levels will view them as collaborators, who share their burden to solve the social problems in society and not as competitors.

Consider the trend in the United States under President Obama's leadership. According to him, 'The bottom line is clear. Solutions to America's challenges are being developed every day at the grass roots – and government shouldn't be supplanting those efforts, it should be supporting those efforts.'[2] Under the Obama administration, the United States has worked diligently to live up to this expectation by providing support for social entrepreneurs and supporting innovative collaborations between organizations in the United States and stake-holders in the international arena. More specifically, through the White House Office of Social Innovation and Civic Participation (SICP), the United States government engages the social sector – individuals, nonprofits, foundations – as well as business and state and federal government agencies – to find new ways to solve old problems and drive collaboration. SICP is also focused on strengthening and supporting the social sector by developing policies and programs that can accelerate economic recovery and create stronger communities. Similarly, Challenge.gov[3] is a one-stop shop that has engaged citizens and entrepreneurs to participate in more than 400 public sector prize competitions with over $72 million in prizes.

Sadly, this experience is not shared across Africa. Some governments in Africa have introduced competitions, innovation funds, challenges grants, incubators, technology parks and accelerators, in partnership with the private sector and civil society to spur social entrepreneurship and innovation. However, these inter-ventions are often short-lived and have achieved mixed results, with many countries neglecting to shape policy on critical issues, such as intellectual property protection, to ensure that the innovations developed through these channels can survive and even thrive.

Ultimately, every social entrepreneur's dream is that the government partners with them to scale their proven business models as has been the case with AHI and ESSPIN outlined in Chapter 5. Sadly, there are not enough examples of this practice in Africa. Many governments still prefer to develop and implement their own interventions, which are often more expensive and not as effective or sustainable as scaling proven business models.

Governments also need to actively partner and fund social innovations which address critical gaps in social services. Riders for Health's success across

Africa has proven that this model is possible. However, there is need for greater government engagement in funding key innovations similar to the trend in the United States, where state governments have funded charter schools. These schools are providing disadvantaged children with high quality education, and achieving remarkable impact. Similarly, social impact bonds, which were first launched in the United Kingdom and are being attempted in Mozambique, will serve as a very useful intervention for more governments to 'pay for performance' and to achieve pre-agreed milestones linked to critical social problems.

In summary, national and regional governments should support the scaling of social innovations by:

Revamping the educational sector

As identified in Chapter 3, 'Talent for Scaling', one of the biggest constraints faced by social innovators in Africa is human capital. Governments in Africa have an important role to play in strengthening the educational systems at the local, state and federal levels in all countries. In addition to basic skills, upgrading the curriculum to incorporate science, technology, engineering, arts and mathematics as well as social entrepreneurship and life skills such as creativity, risk-taking, networking, negotiations and communications is critical for preparing a capable and committed workforce. This investment will benefit all sectors and will create the next generation of social innovators on the continent.

Creating an enabling environment for social innovators to thrive

This includes creating, implementing and monitoring regulatory policies and support programs that encourage and protect social enterprises, nonprofits and hybrids and enable them to achieve social impact. For example, governments can create a social innovation desk in each critical social service ministry to identify high-impact social innovations in the public, private, and nonprofit sectors and actively support their scaling in partnership with the founders, the private sector and development partners. Priority ministries include health, education, agriculture and energy.

They should also invest in strengthening in-country national research capabilities to ensure regular and credible census, and human development reports which would provide effective baselines for measuring changes to the social and economic landscape.

In addition, they should provide effective regulations, including clear and transparent reporting requirements for social businesses and nonprofits to minimize fraud and maximize impact. Policies and regulations should ensure that products and inputs that are imported into their countries for scaling efforts are safe and of high quality. Governments should also implement regulations that foster a level playing field for local and international NGOs.

Creating and implementing laws, regulations and incentives which encourage companies, communities and individuals to invest in, donate to and partner with social enterprises

Local and international impact investors need to be assured of a stable macro and microeconomic environment where they make their investments. As outlined in the framework developed by the Global Impact Investing Policy Project, African governments have a critical role to play in defining and monitoring the implementation of investment rules and requirements. They need to develop and implement policies focused on taxes, subsidies, reporting requirements, including setting guidelines for banks and institutional investors to articulate the social and environmental impact of their investments and enable appropriate corporate structures. For example, the pioneering Regulation 28 of the Pension Funds Act in South Africa includes a provision for pension funds to invest in responsible vehicles, including a requirement that incorporates environmental, social and governance (ESG) factors into the investment decision-making process.

In terms of participation, governments can co-invest directly or through private equity vehicles, as is the case with the Fund for Agriculture Financing in Nigeria, procure services as is the case with Riders for Health; and build capacity through the creation or support of education institutions, incubators, clusters, and hubs.

African governments need to create personal and corporate tax incentives

Individuals and companies that support social causes should receive tax incentives. Clearly this can only be accomplished in an environment where there are high levels of tax compliance and the systems and structures are sophisticated enough to track and identify false claims.

Governments should also create incentives, including tax breaks or processing equipment importation duty waivers for companies that invest in or source their raw materials in the country, via inclusive business models. These incentives can also apply to companies that offer services to rural communities through significant infrastructural investments.

Leveraging public resources and infrastructure to actively support and partner with social entrepreneurs to scale high-impact interventions

African governments need to gradually reduce their engagement in the provision of services which other private and civil society organizations are better equipped to deliver, with higher impact and at lower costs. In addition, following the examples of ESSPIN and AHI, they should support the scale up of proven models by civil society or private groups or the creation of new policies to enshrine proven methodologies or ideologies into the law.

Bright Simmons, mPedigree's Founder, best captured this recommendation in interview for this book with his sentiments,

Governments in Africa need to completely re-orient national research and development budgets away from the out-of-touch early post-independence national research institutes into a more 'national innovation accelerator' type dispensation that connects with young entrepreneurs and innovators from both business and academia. 'National innovation systems' need to be viewed in less abstract terms, and dominant actors should be compelled through local content legislation to report progress in supporting innovation accelerators across multiple domains, departments, agencies, sectors, and operations of the public sector.

Investing in infrastructure development, especially in rural areas

The huge disparity between the basic amenities that are available to the rural poor across sub-Saharan Africa invariably affects the ability of social innovators to scale in rural communities. African governments need to become more transparent and accountable about their infrastructure investments, specifically the feeder road networks, which enable more farmers to access markets, the grid and off-grid solutions and internet connectivity, and partner with the private sector and civil society to invest in infrastructural development.

Development partners

As explored through the numerous case examples outlined in this book, development partners have a critical role to play as catalysts, facilitators and funders for scaling social innovation in Africa. They can and often do support governments in creating an enabling environment for high-impact social innovations to thrive. This role is even more important under autocratic regimes, which typically crack down on the social sector. In these situations, development partners often serve to protect or shield key actors in the social sector, enabling them to fight against tyranny and for the rights of the masses.

Development partners also fund academia to conduct research and provide subsidized courses for social innovators. In addition, they host and fund conferences focused on social innovations, and support challenge funds, prizes, innovation funds and fellowships, as explored through the preceding chapters in this book.

Traditional and new foundations and investors are supporting the emergence of social entrepreneurs across Africa through multi-sector initiatives targeted at providing start-up and growth funding, customized support services, executive education, and advisory services.

Development partners also engage in supporting networks within sectors. For example, the Center for Health Market Innovations (CHMI), managed by Results for Development (R4D), is supported by the Bill & Melinda Gates Foundation, the Rockefeller Foundation and UK-AID. It promotes 'programs, policies and practices that make quality health care delivered by private organizations affordable and accessible to the world's poor.'[4] More specifically,

CHMI identifies innovative programs and policies, analyses them to determine which practices can be scaled or adapted in other countries and connects key stakeholders including founders, implementers and funders to provide the required support for scaling. As of May 2015, over 1,400 initiatives have been listed on the CHMI database.

R4D has also launched the Center for Education Innovations, with hubs in South Africa, Kenya and Nigeria, and the Social Accountability Atlas to track and enhance public spending and service delivery.

Despite their successes, there are many top-down, donor-designed approaches to supporting initiatives, which are focused on donor-driven priorities instead of local needs. In fact, many development partners outsource large ticket projects to development consulting and project management companies from their home countries, with limited involvement of local innovators or partners. This typically results in short-lived interventions, with these initiatives dying when the funding ends. In addition, there is often poor coordination among development partners to maximize collaborations and minimize overlaps, which in turn leads to wastage of resources. They are also more willing to fund pilots and roll-outs, with limited regard for scale or sustainability.

Going forward, in order to truly support the scaling of social impact in Africa, development partners need to:

Support governments in their efforts to create an enabling environment

Development partners can fund some of the interventions outlined above, including policies and programs that support growth, strengthening of national research institutions for credible data and policies and frameworks that foster local impact investments and donations or grants from companies and individuals. Where needed, development partners should actively protect social innovators, especially from governments that are hostile.

More specifically, the World Bank, through its annual 'Doing Business' report and the World Economic Forum's 'Global Competitiveness' report, which track and rank the enabling environments for businesses by countries, should include indicators specifically focused on social innovation and scaling. This will further propel governments to actively work towards creating an enabling environment for scaling.

Invest in research

There is clearly a significant gap in local research on social innovations on the African continent, including baseline data on key sectors, the activities of local social innovators operating at the grass roots, the impact of initiatives that are scaling, and lessons from failures. Development partners should provide funding to local organizations to conduct research and knowledge management on social innovation in a systematic and sustainable way. They should also fund the dissemination of this research to ensure impact.

Partner with more local organizations

Use local organizations to design and fund relevant and timely, demand-driven interventions and ensure the sustainability of funded initiatives by requiring that grantee or partner organizations outline **clear scaling and sustainability strategies** for every new project or program. In addition, development partners need to invest in building the capacity of local organizations, specifically in the areas of financial management, measurement and evaluation and knowledge management to enable them to become 'investment-ready'.

Support the emergence of Africa-wide social innovator networks

The networks should focus on key sectors such as agriculture, energy, education and health, which also foster collaboration across sectors. In addition, development partners should invest in capacity building through the support and strengthening of more schools for social entrepreneurship in Africa's leading universities, similar to the Bertha Centre for Social Innovation and Entrepreneurship of the University of Cape Town in South Africa.

Development partners should resist the urge to continue to fund only the donor darlings, and **actively invest in finding local innovators and supporting their scaling efforts**. This process requires that funders broaden and deepen their pipeline of local innovators by tapping into in-country networks of social innovators, such as LEAP's Annual Social Innovators Program, and the more than 200 local innovation spaces across Africa. Instead of waiting for internet-savvy innovators to find them, funders should request for referrals from traditional funders such as Ford Foundation, which has supported social innovators in Africa for more than 60 years, and Ashoka, which has a grass roots reach. Traditional private-equity firms, which are members of the African Venture Capital & Private Equity Association have a strong presence on the ground, and can also support early screening and due diligence efforts. Development partners should attend and participate in the growing number of Maker Faire and business-plan competitions on the continent, and support the introduction of innovation labs and formal training programs in universities and vocational schools to inspire and equip the next generation of African social innovators. They should also work with local organizations to collate and disseminate information about global support opportunities for local innovators, using technology.

Actively engage in local, national and regional donor work groups

Work groups ensure robust collaborations with other funders. They foster more targeted interventions in sectors or regions that are neglected and enable streamlining of activities, a reduction of duplication of efforts and enhance impact. For example, the Development Partners Group in Tanzania was formally established in 2004[5] and is composed of 17 bilateral and five multilateral institutions. It focuses on ensuring effective, transparent and accountable country systems; increasing coordination and harmonization among donors; and reinforcing mutual accountability. It has five distinct clusters, including the Education Group which is focused on increasing access to education, enhancing the quality of education, and the institutional capacity of Tanzania's education sector. This Partners Group actively tracks individual and collective impact and has been able to demonstrate significant results through a close partnership with the Tanzanian government. There is an urgent need for similar interventions in other African countries and within priority sectors.

There is also an urgent need for a strong community of home-grown philanthropists that can work collaboratively to support social innovations. Organizations such as the African Philanthropy Forum, established by the Global Philanthropy Forum and Trust Africa are leading efforts to address this gap.

Private sector

The private sector in Africa has an important role to play in supporting social entrepreneurs, whether they are nonprofit or for-profit ventures. It invests in social enterprises via strategic partnerships and impact investments. This trend is evident across Africa in varying degrees because there is growing recognition that it is possible to do well and do good at the same time.

The private sector across Africa also integrates social enterprises into its operations by providing support that makes strategic sense for business. This approach, often described as 'inclusive business', typically involves social enterprises managing outgrower schemes or bottom-of-the pyramid distribution models on behalf of the large company or leveraging the extensive distribution channels and supply chain networks of the corporation or private company to enhance their scale and impact.

The private sector also engages social innovators as part of a corporate social responsibility (CSR) initiative or through their foundations. This includes providing financial and in-kind support, including employee engagement in volunteer activities for the social sector.

Companies such as Danone are actively engaged in corporate impact venturing in Africa. Danone currently manages three funds – the Danone Communities Fund, which encourages social innovation around last-mile distribution, the Danone Ecosystem Fund, which provides grants to improve business practices across its value chains, and the Livelihoods Fund, focused on carbon sequestration in low-income rural communities. In Senegal, Danone Communities supported Bagoré Bathily, a young Senegalese veterinarian and the founder of La Laiterie du Berger to scale his dairy business, based on the unique dairy development program model. In addition, by investing in the company and providing technical assistance in product formulation, marketing and production, the company dramatically enhanced its milk collection and yogurt processing capabilities three-fold. It now sources milk from over 600 families of cattle herders, enabling them to settle around the processing facility and improve their livelihoods.

Finally the private sector assists social enterprises to build their brands and tell their stories. Traditional and social media have played a critical role in telling the stories of social entrepreneurs, showcasing their impact or failures, and changing mindsets about the landscape of social innovation. This role has to be further enhanced to continue to shape paradigms about the social sector.

In spite of the positive trends highlighted above regarding private sector support of scaling efforts, it is important to recognize these practices are not widely adopted across the continent, and that there is an urgent need for systematic and sustained private sector engagement. More specifically, in order to truly support the scaling of social innovations, the private sector in Africa needs to:

Provide impact investments and catalytic funds

Similar to the example of Danone cited above, more indigenous African companies need to actively invest in scaling social innovations. In addition, the African private sector needs to expand beyond its comfort zone of working with the popular and proven nonprofits to find and partner with credible organizations solving social problems at the grassroots. It also needs to dramatically shift from marketing and public relations, masked as corporate social responsibility, to deepen its strategic partnerships with social innovators to solve social problems.

Invest in reaching the unbanked via innovative financial products, providing off-grid solutions to populations without electricity and internet connectivity to rural areas

Sadly, too many financial institutions, energy, telecommunications and internet service providers in Africa choose to restrict their activities to cities and towns, with widespread neglect of rural communities, which they deem unprofitable and difficult to serve. This strategy is very short-term focused and underestimates the immense potential of the rural areas to generate income, especially given the important role of agriculture as a key growth sector across the continent. Visionary private sector organizations, including banks, microfinance and other financial institutions have a critical role to play in extending services to the unbanked, to enable them to actively engage in the broad-range of opportunities for payments and crowd-funding. Similarly, energy companies, especially those engaged in off-grid solutions – including solar – can generate significant results by working in rural communities.

Partner with social innovators to build inclusive value and supply chains and distribution channels

Thankfully, a few governments are beginning to exert significant pressure on or provide incentives for large companies operating in Africa to source more of their raw materials locally to contribute to the economy and promote job creation. Regardless of whether or not there is pressure or any incentive from the government, large private companies in Africa should collaborate with social innovators to develop and implement strategic raw material sourcing and distribution strategies for low-income populations.

Amplify the impact of social innovators via the provision of pro bono support and encouraging employees to serve as volunteers for social sector initiatives

Human resource executives globally argue that employee loyalty to any company increases when it gives them the opportunity to volunteer for and support causes that are meaningful. Clearly, this spirit of volunteerism and pro bono contributions needs to be encouraged by more private companies in Africa. In return, social innovators have to ensure that the volunteers enjoy a fulfilling and meaningful experience and are treated with respect and a high degree of professionalism. They also have to quantify the financial value of this support and ensure that the private company feels valued and appreciated, through appropriate recognitions on the social enterprises website, publications and other media, as appropriate.

Participate in global, regional and national networks that promote engagement with social innovators

This participation will expose more African private companies to best practices and global partners who can support their efforts to promote social innovation. For example, the Global Impact Investing Network (GIIN) supports the development of and raises awareness about the emerging field of impact investing by building a strong network of investors and leaders, with a growing number in Africa. Similarly, the Aspen Network of Development Entrepreneurs (ANDE), a global network of organizations that propel entrepreneurship in emerging markets, with a presence in West and East Africa, provides support to members such as business development service providers, impact investors and academic institutions, all focused on entrepreneurship.

Academia

Since the mid-1990s, social enterprise centres have emerged at leading global universities, including Harvard Business School, Berkeley, Oxford, Stanford, Yale, Georgetown, and a range of other universities in the Americas and Europe. These centres have played an important role in conducting research on the sector, sharing best practices, engaging students in internships and full-time positions in the social entrepreneurship sector, and supporting them to start their own ventures via business plan competitions and funding support. These efforts have fostered the emergence of an army of social entrepreneurs, who are tackling some of the world's most difficult problems, and those who are willing to support them.

In addition, beyond engaging students and executives via the social enterprise centres and shaping their experiences, a few academic institutions actually collaborate with communities to spur local social entrepreneurship. For example, the MIT D-Lab, through its creative capacity building methodology, identifies and supports social entrepreneurs in their communities. The D-Lab's program in Uganda allowed MIT to meet and support Betty Ikalany, the Executive Director of Teso Women Development Initiatives, who has pioneered and is scaling innovations focused on using agricultural waste in Uganda to create charcoal and clean stoves. These types of grass roots engagements are critical to deepening the emergence of local social entrepreneurs across Africa.

It is important to note that apart from the University of Cape Town's Bertha Centre for Social Innovation, there are no other universities in sub-Saharan Africa with centres focused on social innovation and entrepreneurship. However, countries such as Nigeria have introduced entrepreneurship education as a critical component of every university degree, actively managed by the National Universities Commission. While this type of intervention is a welcome development, in the face of growing youth unemployment, universities must ensure that high-quality and practical training is provided to the students, leveraging volunteer entrepreneurs from the private sector. They should also explicitly incorporate social entrepreneurship as a component of the broader entrepreneurship coursework.

Indeed, academia in Africa has a critical role to play in supporting the social sector by:

Incorporating social innovation into broad-based entrepreneurship and Science, Technology, Engineering, Art & Mathematics (STEAM) education

All business and STEAM faculties at the undergraduate and graduate levels in Africa should include modules on social innovation into their curriculum. Working through platforms such as the Association of African Business Schools and the Association of African Universities, all members can benefit from exposure to relevant curriculum, training for faculty, and best practices for providing practical education to students via field projects, business plan competitions and fellowships and internships imbedded in social enterprises. Ultimately, this will not only enrich the experiences of the students, but will also create an army of capable and competent change agents and social innovators for the continent.

Promoting executive education for social innovators and incorporating courses on the social sector for participants from the public and private sectors

This is needed in order to foster knowledge sharing and collaboration. There is tremendous potential for key actors from the government, development community, private sector, and academia to partner and strengthen the social sector in Africa and address many of the challenges that limit its ability to serve as a strong 'third sector' – truly filling the gaps that others cannot.

Strengthening research and knowledge management on social innovation

Academia in Africa has a critical role to play in documenting the successes and failures of African social innovators, and in sharing them widely to strengthen individual organizations, and the entire sector. This material can also be used as curriculum for teaching students and executives about the social sector. It can support the development of tailored measurement and evaluation tools and the independent assessments of the impact of social innovations. Finally, academia can partner with leading academic institutions in the United States and Europe to jointly prepare case studies and publications to showcase the work of African social innovators on the global stage.

Actively engaging students in field and volunteer projects

This will ensure that students are focused on social change to enhance their commitment to service and to groom the next generation of social entrepreneurs. Industrial attachments and internships are a critical part of education in the twenty-first century, where students gain practical experience and exposure to the 'world of work', which invariably shapes their perspectives and prepares them to select meaningful careers. As a result, academic institutions in Africa should work diligently through career services departments to match deserving students with high-impact social innovators in their communities or countries, who they can support in a mutually beneficial relationship.

Civil society

Africa desperately needs a strong civil society, that is recognized as credible and transparent, which can hold governments, the development community and the private sector accountable and ensure that they deliver on many of the recommendations outlined above. In addition, there is an urgent need for stronger collaborations between civil society organizations within sectors and countries, across regions, the continent and the global community. These collaborations and linkages play a critical role in strengthening the individual and collective efforts of the organizations engaged. They also amplify their individual voices and strengthen their collective bargaining power, enabling them to jointly advocate for changes in policy, shape ecosystems and enhance their collective impact. Finally, civil society in Africa can serve as invaluable partners for social innovators, by amplifying the methodologies and ideologies of high-impact social interventions, mobilizing grass roots support and spreading them through wide networks, including faith-based, community, trade and industry associations.

In order to play these critical roles, organizations operating in Africa's civil society have to strengthen their systems, structures, and controls for managing their budgets and cash flow. They also have to build ethical organizations to reflect the high level of integrity, accountability, and transparency that is required to sustain public trust and deliver high-impact results.

Other support structures: incubators, hubs, accelerators and technology parks

In addition to the key roles that the public, and private sectors, the development community, academia and civil society can and should play in fostering the scaling of social innovations, there are emerging support structures which cut across these sectors, and complete their efforts. They include incubators, hubs, accelerators and technology parks.

Incubators

Incubators typically play a critical role in nurturing new innovators and social entrepreneurs and providing them with the systems, structures and support required to pilot and commence the scaling process. There are over 200[6] innovation and incubator spaces on the African continent, operating at varying levels of sophistication and with mixed results. Examples of high-impact incubators in sub-Saharan Africa include the Co-Creation Hub (CcHUB) in Lagos, Nigeria, which has birthed a range of successful social innovations, including the award-winning BudgIT. The idea behind BudgIT was actually conceptualized during the Tech-In-Governance, a gathering organized by Co-Creation Hub in February 2011. BudgIT empowers citizens with critical information about the government and its budget and spending patterns. It provides valuable government data to the general public via mobile and online solutions, including simple tweets, interactive formats or infographic displays. Through its pioneering work, BudgIT has raised broad-based awareness, spurred public dialogues and debates and led behaviour change in the public sector.

In addition, Ushahidi, initially developed in 2008 to map reports of violence in Kenya after the post-election fallout, also created the iHub, which has more than 14,000 members and has incubated 150 tech startups.

Initially started with donor funding, many of the incubators in Africa are gradually becoming self-sufficient, especially through earned income generated from their hubs and the equity stakes that some of them are starting to take in promising start-ups.

Technology parks

Technology parks have been established in Africa to enhance sharing of ideas and promote innovation. They focus on a range of sectors including agriculture, ICT, energy and healthcare. These technology parks are funded by governments and development partners such as United Nations Industrial Development Organization (UNIDO), and United Nations Educational, Scientific and Cultural Organization (UNESCO).[7] Technology parks on the continent include Technopark Africa in Cote D'Ivoire, Technopole du Toamasina in Madagascar, Technopole de Dakar & Dakar Technopolis (DTP) in Senegal,[8] Kigali ICT park in Rwanda, National University of Science and Technology Technopark (NUST) in Zimbabwe, and Technopark Stellenbosch, Softline Technology Park (STP),

Highveld Techno Park (HTP), Innovation Hub Science Park (IHSP), Pretoria, Coega Technology Park (CTP), Port Elizabeth, all in South Africa.[9]

Accelerators

Accelerators provide business model development, financial analysis, supply chain and sourcing, market access and distribution, linkages and mentoring support to innovators. A 2013 landscaping exercise conducted by The Rockefeller Foundation and Monitor Deloitte revealed that there are more than 160[10] accelerators operating in the United States, sub-Saharan Africa (SSA), and Southeast Asia.

With primary operations in the US, Unreasonable Institute and Village Capital both support African innovators. For example, Village Capital provides a 12-week program, consisting of lectures and group projects, with only 20 entrepreneurs selected for each session.

On the continent, the Social Franchise Accelerator, which is a collaboration of three organizations – the International Centre for Social Franchising, the Bertha Centre for Social Innovation and Entrepreneurship and Franchising Plus, provides support to innovators working to implement a franchise model.

Clearly, there is definitely a need for more accelerators on the African continent, specifically focused on key sectors, such as agriculture, energy, health and education.

Summary

Key stakeholders, including governments, development partners, private sector and civil society, all have critical roles to play in supporting the scaling of social innovations on the African continent. More specifically, governments need to work independently and collaboratively to create an enabling environment, including implementing laws, regulations and incentives which encourage companies, communities and individuals to invest in social innovations. They also need to leverage public resources and infrastructure to actively support and partner with social entrepreneurs to scale high-impact interventions. Development partners need to invest in building the capacity of more African social innovators to ensure that they are 'investment ready' and actively fund scaling, measurement and evaluation and sustainability strategies for initiatives. They also need to support the emergence of Africa-wide social innovator networks and join more donor collaboration groups to streamline and strengthen their engagement in Africa. The private sector needs to push beyond CSR to form strategic partnerships with social innovators, and extend the reach of the services to rural communities. Academia has to incorporate social innovation into broad-based entrepreneurship and STEAM education and conduct research on the sector and its impact. Civil society also has to hold the key actors accountable for implementing these critical recommendations. Finally, incubators, technology parks and accelerators, which cut across a range of the stakeholders identified above also have an important role in supporting scaling.

Notes

1   Jack William, Suri Tavneet, *The Economics of M PESA*, Georgetown University and MIT Sloan, August, 2010. *10 Myths About M-Pesa*, 2014; www.cgap.org/blog/10-myths-about-m-pesa-2014-update. *Why does Kenya lead the world in mobile money?* May 27th 2013; Economist Blogs www.economist.com/blogs/economist-explains/2013/05/economist-explains-18

2   White House website, accessed April 10, 2015; www.whitehouse.gov/administration/eop/sicp

3   Challenge.gov website, accessed June 20, 2015, www.challenge.gov

4   Health Market Innovations website, accessed October 1, 2015; http://healthmarket innovations.org/

5   Development Partners Group Tanzania website, accessed August 10, 2015; www.tzdpg.or.tz/dpg-website/dpg-tanzania.html

6   Public List of African Innovation Spaces, Googledocs, https://docs.google.com/spreadsheets/d/1DvXVB2ikFzUxi78lznojlZyDcR_Gn43i7m-Y3mkTrCQ/edit#gid=0

7   UNESCO website, accessed March 14, 2015; www.unesco.org/new/en/natural sciences/science-technology/sti-policy/africa/creation-of-a-pilot-science-park-in-an-african-country/

8   UNIDO website, accessed March 10, 2015; www.unido.org/en/how-we-work/convening-partnerships-and-networks/networks-centres-forums-and-platforms/technology-parks/mapping/africa-sub-sahara-region/senegal.html

9   UNESCO website, accessed on March 14, 2015; www.unesco.org/new/en/natural-sciences/science-technology/university-industry-partnerships/science-parks-around-the-world/science-parks-in-africa/

10 *Accelerating Impact Exploring Best Practices, Challenges, and Innovations in Impact Enterprise Acceleration*, February 2015, Monitor Deloitte, Funded by the Rockefeller Foundation.

7 Looking to the future for social innovators

2015 marked the official end of the Millennium Development Goals (MDGs) era. From their inception, African presidents and their citizens embraced these goals with varying levels of intensity. According to the *MDG Report 2015, Assessing Progress in Africa toward the Millennium Development Goals*,[1] while countries in sub-Saharan Africa were able to achieve some critical targets including increasing women's representation in national parliaments, reducing infant and HIV-related deaths, and enhancing access to primary schooling, many others were unmet. Importantly, goals of poverty reduction and improved child nutrition were unrealized.

Overall, the report suggests that progress was slower in meeting the needs of the hardest-to-reach populations on the continent such as out-of-school youth, children with disabilities and living in conflict affected States, nomadic people, rural communities and some ethnic minorities. It also notes that the Ebola crisis which ravaged Guinea, Sierra Leone and Liberia from 2014 to 2015, demonstrated how quickly progress can unravel when systems are not resilient to shocks. In addition, the report exposes the data challenges facing national statistical systems and underscores the importance of strengthening statistical and analytical capacities. Finally, it concludes with the same premise as this book – that 'moving forward, countries will benefit from continued support to develop home-grown solutions to development challenges'.[2]

The sad reality on the continent is that even though there are a growing number of home-grown social innovations, there are too few examples that have scaled. Through this book, I have attempted to equip aspiring and emerging social innovators and their ecosystem of support networks with the knowledge and tools to scale. The book lays out the building blocks for achieving impact at scale by creating clear mission, vision and values statements, and business models that are demand-driven, simple, low-cost, with compelling measurement and evaluation tools that leverage technology. It also explores the steps for attracting and retaining talent and financing and forming strategic partnerships with the private, public and nonprofit sectors to foster scaling. Finally, it outlines concrete action steps for key stakeholders to take in order to support the emergence of more social innovators on the African continent, create an enabling environment for the scaling of high-impact initiatives and advancing our collective efforts to build stronger communities for current and future generations of Africans.

I recognize that social innovators will continue to struggle to scale in our context unless we address the root causes and systematic hurdles that continue to limit development in Africa. This includes the need for democratic governance, the rule of law, transparent and accountable governments at the local, state and national levels, strong institutions in the public sector – especially our legal, judicial, legislative and electoral systems – and vibrant and ethical private and nonprofit sectors. We need domestic resource mobilization and public expenditure management, and credible, effective and dynamic national statistical systems. In addition, we require a transparent and effective civil society that holds the government accountable and an empowered and educated population that understands its rights and demonstrates the values of integrity and hard work required to collectively transform our countries and continent. We also need a more unified Africa, with greater communication and collaboration across borders, increased trade, strengthened cooperation in stemming illicit outflows and returning stolen assets, a strong community of homegrown philanthropists and enhanced support for scaling high-impact social interventions.

Indeed, it is our primary responsibility to build the Africa of our dreams – where every child can live in a peaceful and safe environment, benefit from nutritious food sourced locally, high-quality education and healthcare, and grow up to fulfill his or her highest potential.

With the new set of development targets, sustainable development goals (SDGs), there is a renewed sense of opportunity and hope. Even though the list appears even more daunting than the MDGs, there are at least three key differences between 2000 and 2015 which make me considerably more optimistic about our ability to achieve them in our lifetime.

BOX 7.1: SUSTAINABLE DEVELOPMENT GOALS (SDGs)

- End poverty in all its forms everywhere.
- End hunger, achieve food security and improved nutrition and promote sustainable agriculture.
- Ensure healthy lives and promote well-being for all at all ages.
- Ensure inclusive and equitable quality education and promote lifelong learning opportunities for all.
- Achieve gender equality and empower all women and girls.
- Ensure availability and sustainable management of water and sanitation for all.
- Ensure access to affordable, reliable, sustainable and modern energy for all.
- Promote sustained, inclusive and sustainable economic growth, full and productive employment and decent work for all.

- Build resilient infrastructure, promote inclusive and sustainable industrialization and foster innovation.
- Reduce inequality within and among countries.
- Make cities and human settlements inclusive, safe, resilient and sustainable.
- Ensure sustainable consumption and production patterns.
- Take urgent action to combat climate change and its impacts.
- Conserve and sustainably use the oceans, seas and marine resources for sustainable development.
- Protect, restore and promote sustainable use of terrestrial ecosystems, sustainably manage forests, combat desertification, and halt and reverse land degradation and halt biodiversity loss.
- Promote peaceful and inclusive societies for sustainable development, provide access to justice for all and build effective, accountable and inclusive institutions at all levels.
- Strengthen the means of implementation and revitalize the global partnership for sustainable development.

Source: The United Nations website; accessed November 30 2015. www.un.org/sustainabledevelopment/sustainable-development-goals/

First, propelled by the rapid growth in cellular phone usage and the spread of the internet, the information, communications and technology landscape in Africa is radically different than it was fifteen years ago. This essentially empowers every citizen who has a cell phone to take a photo or send a message which could expose fraud in a matter of seconds. Technology also enhances our ability to collect data for measuring impact, provide training, share best practices and ultimately, increases the speed and reduce the cost of scaling.

Second, the rise of social innovation on the African continent and the growing ecosystem of funders, facilitators and enablers to support them as demonstrated by some of the case studies captured in this book, reveal that there is an emerging army of change agents. Coupling these two perspectives, consider the example of the Kaduna State government in Nigeria which has established a formal relationship with BudgIT, to launch an open budgeting system which will enable citizens to see the policies, budgets, procurement records and also status of fund releases in a single space. According to Oluseun Onigbinde of BudgIT, 'Citizens will be able to verify and monitor the government's progress using their mobile phones, and can report their feedback via the platform'.[3] Pioneering efforts led by Kaduna State in partnership with BudgIT demonstrate the potential impact that can be achieved when credible and committed public sector leaders collaborate with social innovators to change ecosystems.

Third, Africa's private sector is growing, creating its share of millionaires and billionaires. These individuals and their companies have a greater understanding of the importance of philanthropy and the critical need for strategic collaborations across sectors to address social problems. They are engaging in a more systematic manner with social innovators to jointly support scaling efforts. If channeled appropriately, this has the potential to significantly reduce the dependency of African social innovators on international funders.

Clearly, we have just scratched the surface of our social change efforts. However, I am more convinced today than when I embarked on the journey of inquiry into scaling social innovation in Africa, that we can feed, educate, provide healthcare, housing, sanitation, transportation and create jobs for billions of Africans that will be born between now and 2030. Through scaling social innovations in education and family planning, we may even be able to stem the population tide.

I challenge you to imbibe the words of Nelson Mandela – 'Vision without action is just a dream, action without vision just passes the time, and vision with action can change the world'.

Africa needs our vision and action for meaningful and sustainable change to occur. The future of many generations depends on our willingness to go beyond just transforming our ideas into reality, but diligently and collaboratively create a level of scale that can truly transform Africa into the brighter and more equitable continent that we all envision.

Notes

1   *MDG Report 2015: Assessing Progress in Africa toward the Millennium Development Goals*, developed by the United Nations Economic Commission for Africa, African Union, African Development Bank and United Nations Development Program, www.undp. org/content/undp/en/home/librarypage/mdg/mdg-reports/africa-collection.html

2   *MDG Report 2015: Assessing Progress in Africa toward the Millennium Development Goals*, developed by the United Nations Economic Commission for Africa, African Union, African Development Bank and United Nations Development Program.

3   'Kaduna, BudgIT partner on Open Budget System', Premium Times website, June 27, 2015; www.premiumtimesng.com/news/more-news/185725-kaduna-budgit-partner-on-open-budget-system.html

Appendices

Funding sources for social innovators

Name of intiative	Sector focus and activities	Presence/activities in Africa	Website address
Acumen Fund	Offers economic development and poverty alleviation through impact investing	Offices in Accra and Nairobi. Active in West and East Africa where its investments are at the forefront of increasing access to products and services for low-income consumers. Has invested in over 29 companies operating in the African region as of 2015	www.acumen.org
Allan Gray Orbis Foundation	Generates venture capital for entrepreneurial ventures through e2 program	South Africa, Namibia, Botswana and Swaziland	www.allangray orbis.org
Ashoka	Offers seed funding, customized support services, global network, impact investment	African offices in Egypt, Kenya, Nigeria, Senegal, South Africa, Uganda, approximately 405 African fellows as of 2015. Most represented countries: South Africa (109) Nigeria (81), Kenya (37), Uganda (24), Zimbabwe (15)	www.ashoka.org

Name of intiative	Sector focus and activities	Presence/activities in Africa	Website address
Barr Foundation	Gives grants to organizations focused on improving the lives of children and families living in poverty in developing countries	Started a developing country focus program in 2015 with $35 million in grant commitments with a focus on East Africa, India and Haiti. This program ended in 2015	www.barr foundation.org/ global
Baring Foundation	Provided grants to UK international NGOs to capacity build African NGOs and community-based organizations in the area of long-term forced migration from 2001 to 2013. Instituted a new international program in 2015 for locally-based civil society organizations working to address discrimination based on gender, sexual orientation or gender identity in sub-Saharan Africa.		www.baring foundation.org.uk
Bertha Foundation	The Bertha Foundation is a family foundation that works with inspiring leaders who are catalysts for social and economic change	Southern Africa	www.bertha foundation.org/
Bill & Melinda Gates Foundation	Provides grants to support initiatives in global health, agriculture, poverty alleviation and education	Offices in Ethiopia, Nigeria and South Africa. Has made substantial grants in Africa in the areas of agricultural development, poverty alleviation and health	www.gates foundation.org
Big Bang Philanthropy	Is a group of like-minded funders who are working together to find and finance organizations tackling the most pressing problems of the poor	Has funded social enterprises and non-profits extensively across Africa. Member organizations include Last Mile Health, Off-Grid Electric, Muso among others	www.bigbang philantrophy.com
Bloom Foundation	Focuses on the prevention and relief of poverty in the UK and in the developing countries of Africa and Asia. Makes grants and investments into programs and investments focusing on education, health, and self-sustaining solutions		No website

Name of intiative	Sector focus and activities	Presence/activities in Africa	Website address
Bohemian Foundation	Provides grants to support organizations that address some of the serious global challenges in health, poverty, and the environment	Provides grants directly and through other grant-making organizations like the Draper Richards Kaplan Foundation and Echoing Green	www.bohemian foundation.org
Cartier Charitable Foundation	Strives to improve the livelihoods of the most vulnerable, especially women. Focus areas include access to basic services, emergency response, natural resources management and women's social and economic development	Provides grants to partners in its focus areas. Has supported initiatives in Nigeria, Ghana, South Sudan and Ethiopia among others.	www.cartier charitable foundation.org
Case Foundation	Provides grants and impact investments in initiatives that are focused on revolutionizing philanthropy, unleashing entrepreneurship and igniting civic engagement	Contributed $25,000 to a prize pool for entrepreneurs during a pitch event at the Global Entrepreneurship Summit in Nairobi.	www.case foundation.org
Cherie Blair Foundation	Works in partnership with nonprofit, private and public sector organizations, to develop projects with sustainable solutions to the challenges women entrepreneurs face	Has three programs for women: Enterprise Development Program, Mentoring Women in Business Program and Mobile Technology Program	www.cherieblair foundation.org
Children's Investment Fund Foundation	Works with a wide range of partners seeking to transform the lives of poor and vulnerable children in developing countries. Priority areas include health, climate change, nutrition, early learning, deworming and humanitarian efforts	Office in Nairobi. Has supported initiatives extensively across Africa, with over $277 million in grant commitments to Africa	www.ciff.org

Name of intiative	Sector focus and activities	Presence/activities in Africa	Website address
Conrad N. Hilton Foundation	Provides funds to non-profit organizations working to improve the lives of disadvantaged and vulnerable people throughout the world	Has funded initiatives in improving access to safe drinking water, access to affordable microcredit, tackling avoidable blindness, Catholic education and sanitation in a number of African countries including Ethiopia, Zambia, Ghana, Mali and Niger	www.hilton foundation.org
David & Lucile Packard Foundation	Provides grants to organizations and projects in four focus areas: conservation and science, population and reproductive health, children, families and communities	Has invested extensively across Africa, mostly in the population and reproductive health category.	www.packard.org
David Weekly Family Foundation	Provides funding to social enterprises working in the following areas: education, churches, human services and global development. Also open to for-profit investments in companies or funds addressing the bottom billion / base of the pyramid	Involved in microfinance and micro-clinic efforts in Africa. Has provided grant support to One Acre Fund and Hope International in Africa	N/A
Draper Richards Kaplan Foundation	Provides impact investing, seed funding	Seed funding for 27 organizations with operations in Africa including One Acre Fund, Sanergy, West Africa Vocational Initiative and Kiva	www.drk foundation.org

Name of intiative	Sector focus and activities	Presence/activities in Africa	Website address
Eastern Congo Initiative	Founded by Ben Affleck, focuses on creating an Eastern Congo vibrant with opportunities for economic and social development, and where a robust civil society can flourish	Achieves its objectives through two means: advocacy and grant making. Provides grants to Congolese organizations working to advance economic development, maternal and child health, access to justice and access to higher education	www.eastern congo.com
Echoing Green	Provides seed funding and technical assistance to emerging social entrepreneurs with ideas for social change	45 African Fellows as of 2015, the majority working in healthcare and economic development, other common sectors include education and agriculture, most represented countries are Kenya (12) South Africa (6), Uganda (5), Rwanda (4), Nigeria/Liberia (3)	www.echoing green.org
Eleos Foundation	Strives to improve millions of lives by investing in pioneering business solutions to poverty. Provides seed capital, advisory and fundraising services to companies in East Africa, Liberia, India, Central America and the Northern Andean Corridor	Has invested in a number of Kenyan social enterprises including Sanergy, Copia and Eco Fuels Kenya	www.theeleos foundation.com
Elma Growth Foundation	Started in 2013, invests exclusively in African companies that seek to relieve poverty and/or the effects of poverty on individuals, families or communities	Has made 8 investments since inception. Investee companies include African Leadership Academy, Village Health Works, Ashesi University among others	www.elmaphilant hropies.org/ foundation/ the-elma-growth- foundation/

Name of intiative	Sector focus and activities	Presence/activities in Africa	Website address
Flora Family Foundation	Supports public benefit organizations working in education, health, arts and culture, the environment, global security, civic engagement and the advancement of women	Has invested in women advancement initiatives in Tanzania	www.florafamily.org
Ford Foundation	Provides grants to support visionary leaders and organizations on the frontlines of social change across the world.	Offices in Egypt, Nigeria, Kenya and South Africa, Ubuntu Institute for Young Social focuses on Southern Africa	www.fordfoundation.org
Forward Foundation	Provides funding to social start-ups in Ethiopia, Kenya, Uganda and the UK	Has provided over £1.5 million in funding to social startups.	www.forwardfoundation.org.uk
Gatsby Charitable Foundation	Funds and implements programs to accelerate inclusive and sustainable growth in East Africa.	Has funded agricultural finance, local institution building, agricultural research, governance and microfinance initiatives in East Africa	www.gatsby.org.uk
Global Fund for Women	Makes general support grants to women's groups in five regions: sub-Saharan Africa, Middle East and North Africa, Europe and Central Asia, Asia Pacific and Latin America and the Caribbean	Since its inception in 1987, the Global Fund has provided over $100 million to more than 4,400 women's groups in 172 countries.	www.globalfundforwomen.org

Name of intiative	Sector focus and activities	Presence/activities in Africa	Website address
Grameen Foundation	Interventions in poverty alleviation, health and agriculture through microfinance, scaling relevant mobile technology and promoting activities at the community level	Offices in Ghana, Kenya and Uganda. Mobile Technology for Community Health Initiative in Ghana, e-warehouse initiative in Kenya, Africa Health Markets for Equity initiative in Nigeria and Community Knowledge Worker initiative in Uganda	www.grameen foundation.org
IDEO.org	Partners with nonprofit organizations, social enterprises and foundations, to directly address the needs of the poor in sectors like health, water and sanitation, financial inclusion, agriculture and gender equity through design initiatives	Has partnered with a number of nonprofits and social enterprises across Africa. Has completed and ongoing projects in Kenya, Ghana, Tanzania, Ghana and Nigeria	www.ideo.org
IKEA Foundation	Supports programs that aim to create a better everyday life for children living in extreme poverty and refugees	Works primarily through international development organizations like UNICEF, Doctors without Borders, and the Clinton Health Access Initiative among others	www.ikea foundation.org
Indigo Trust	Funds technology-driven projects to bring about social change in African countries. Focused mainly on innovation, transparency, accountability and citizen empowerment initiatives	Has provided grants to over 20 technology driven African social enterprises. Some notable names include CCHub, BudgIT, iCow, Agrohub among others	www.indigotrust. org.uk

Name of intiative	Sector focus and activities	Presence/activities in Africa	Website address
Jasmine Social Investments	Funds entrepreneur-led organizations targeting big problems with market-based approaches	Has funded a number of social enterprises across Africa, including Bridge International Academies, Living Goods, Last Mile Health among others	www.jasmine. org.nz
LGT Venture Philanthropy	Provides impact investments to help organizations making outstanding social and environmental impact scale their operations	Has four active portfolio companies in Africa, three of which are operating in Kenya (2015)	www.lgtvp.com
Lundin Foundation	Provides risk capital, technical assistance, and strategic grants to outstanding social enterprises and organizations across the globe	Had over 15.7 million Canadian dollars in impact investment commitments as at December 31, 2014, the bulk of which is invested in African countries	www.lundin foundation.org
Magnum Foundation (Emergency Fund)	Supports experienced photographers with a commitment to documenting social issues, working long-term, and engaging with an issue over time	Has supported photographers documenting social issues and conflicts in Swaziland, South Africa, Kenya, South Sudan, Egypt and Ethiopia	www.magnum foundation.org/ emergency-fund
Mastercard Foundation	Focuses on helping economically disadvantaged people in Africa out of poverty through programs and initiatives and financial support. Program areas include financial inclusion, education and learning, youth livelihoods and a scholar program	Provides funding for initiatives in its focus program areas through partners such as the US Government, KPMG (Manages the Fund for Rural Prosperity) and Village Capital	www.mastercard fdn.org

Name of intiative	Sector focus and activities	Presence/activities in Africa	Website address
MacArthur Foundation	Works to defend human rights, advance global conservation and security, make cities better places, and understand how technology is affecting children and society	Has provided support for environmental conservation, maternal health and the protection of women's reproductive rights in Kenya, Mozambique and Nigeria	www.macfound. org
Mo Ibrahim Foundation	Established to put governance at the centre of any conversation on African development	Has four initiatives: Ibrahim Index, Ibrahim Prize, Ibrahim Forum and Ibrahim Fellowships	www.moibrahim foundation.org
Montpelier Foundation	Empowers disadvantaged people, supports sustainable and scalable solutions in agriculture, education and training, health, infrastructure, social justice and livelihood creation or improvement	Has provided social impact investments and grants to social enterprises in East Africa	www.montpelier foundation.org.uk
MTN Foundation	Supports initiatives and projects in economic empowerment, education and health	Has implemented a range of interventionist programs and initiatives across Nigeria	foundation.mt nonline.org
Mulago Foundation	Finds and funds high-performance organizations that tackle the basic needs of the very poor	Provides funding for scalable organizations and ideas. Has invested in a number of African initiatives including One Acre Fund, Mothers2Mothers, Sanergy and Wild4Life	www.mulago foundation.org
Nduna Foundation	Makes grants related to preserving human rights in war torn regions in Africa. Also supports efforts in nutrition, food security, pediatric HIV&AIDS and education in developing countries	Has funded projects and nonprofits operating in conflict and post-conflict countries like Niger, Ethiopia, South Sudan, Darfur and Somalia	N/A

Name of intiative	Sector focus and activities	Presence/activities in Africa	Website address
Nike Foundation	Focused on developing adolescent girls into powerful agents of change in the developing world	Works through on-the-ground partners like Mercy Corps in Nigeria to support initiatives on unleashing the 'girl effect' i.e. the power of girls as change agents	www.girleffect.org
Omidyar Network	Impact investments in organizations working to advance social good in the 5 key areas: consumer internet and mobile, education, financial inclusion, governance and citizen engagement, and property rights	Office in Johannesburg. Impact investments in hotels.ng, African Leadership Academy, Bridge International Academies, BudgIT, Paga and Co-Creation Hub among others	www.omidyar.com
Open Road Alliance	Founded in 2012, provides charitable grant capital and recoverable grant capital (low-interest loans) to nonprofits for mid-implementation projects facing an unexpected roadblock or a sudden catalytic opportunity	Has offices in Senegal, Kenya and South Africa, with a strong focus on social justice and economic empowerment.	www.openroad alliance.org
Open Society Foundations (Soros Economic Development Fund)	Supports economic development in post-conflict countries and in nations transitioning to democracy by investing in the financial services, agribusiness, and logistics sectors	Has personnel on the ground in Freetown and Johannesburg. Has invested extensively in agribusiness and financial services across Africa	www.opensociety foundations.org/ about/programs/ soros-economic-development-fund
Pearson Affordable Learning Fund	Makes significant minority equity investments in for-profit companies to meet the growing demand for affordable education across the developing world	Has invested in low-cost school chains in Ghana, Kenya, Nigeria and Tanzania	www.affordable-learning.com

Name of intiative	Sector focus and activities	Presence/activities in Africa	Website address
Peery Foundation	Works to strengthen youth and families and eradicate extreme poverty	Provides grants to social enterprises in Africa, including One Acre Fund, Boma Project and Nuru International	www.peery foundation.org
Pershing Square Foundation	Awards grants and social investments to support exceptional leaders and innovative organizations that tackle important social issues and deliver scalable and sustainable impact.	Has funded social enterprises extensively across Africa. Grantees include Bridge International Academies, Nuru International, myAgro among others	www.pershing squarefoundation. org
Planet Wheeler Foundation	Supports practical and effective projects which make a difference in the alleviation of poverty. Focus areas include education, health, human rights (advocacy & refugees), community development and street kids programs	Founded in 2008. Currently funds over 50 projects in the developing world, 80% of which goes to six regions – East Africa, Burkina Faso, Afghanistan, Burma and Burma related projects	www.planet wheeler.org
Reall – Real Equity For All (Formerly Homeless International)	Dedicated to alleviating living conditions and providing housing and basic services for the urban poor living in slums in Africa and Asia	Provides grants towards initiatives that tackle urban poverty, and provides guarantees and low interest loans to its partners for community-led housing and infrastructure projects in developing regions	www.reall.xyz
Rockefeller Foundation	Provides grants and impact investments to support interventions and innovations in the areas of advancing health, revaluing ecosystems, securing livelihoods and transforming cities	Office in Nairobi. Supports a range of initiatives in Africa including the Alliance for a Green Revolution in Africa (AGRA), Digital Jobs Africa and Africa Impact Economy Innovations Fund (IEIF) Grant Fund	www.rockefeller foundation.org

Name of intiative	Sector focus and activities	Presence/activities in Africa	Website address
Root Capital	Focuses on growing rural prosperity by investing in small and growing agriculture businesses in Africa	Offices in Kenya, Senegal and Uganda. Started investing in East Africa in 2005 and West Africa in 2009	www.rootcapital. org
SAB Foundation	Focuses on igniting a culture of entrepreneurship in South Africa with a focus on women, the youth, persons with disability and persons in rural areas in South Africa	Invests in micro, small and medium enterprises through the SAB Foundation Growth Fund (in partnership with Endeavor), Benevolent private-equity and the Tholoana Enterprise Program	www.sab.co.za/ sablimited/ content/sab foundation-home
Schwab Foundation for Social Entrepreneur- ship	Provides platforms at regional and global level to highlight and advance leading models of sustainable social innovation. Does not make grants	86 fellows running programs in African education (29), technology (27), health (26) (2015)	www.schwab found.org
Segal Family Foundation	Supports outstanding organizations to improve the wellbeing of communities in sub-Saharan Africa, supports these organizations through grants. Focus is on initiatives in adolescent sexual & reproductive health (ASRH) and supporting productive youth	Supports over 180 organizations across 20 countries in sub-Saharan Africa. Has an active team on the ground in East Africa	www.segalfamily foundation.org
Shell Foundation	Aims to catalyze the innovation and scale-up of disruptive new models and technologies that can transform the lives and livelihoods of millions of people	Works across four program areas: access to energy, sustainable mobility, sustainable job change and sustainable supply chains. Regional focus is Africa and Asia. Supports M-KOPA, GroFin and d.light	www.shell foundation.org

Name of intiative	*Sector focus and activities*	*Presence/activities in Africa*	*Website address*
Skoll Foundation	Skoll invests in, connects and celebrates social entrepreneurs and innovators. It provides annual sizeable financial awards to a few social entrepreneurs from across the globe	Skoll has selected a few social innovators operating in Africa for its annual awards	www.skoll.org
Tony Elumelu Foundation	Supports entrepreneurship in Africa through grants and impact investments	Tony Elumelu Foundation Entrepreneurship Programme provides grants and seed capital for new and existing entrepreneurial ventures	www.tonyelumelu foundation.org
TY Danjuma Foundation	Supports initiatives to improve access to health and education and alleviate poverty through grants and other initiatives	Currently operating the Edo and Taraba Community Fund which funds initiatives in its focus areas	www.tydanjuma foundation.org
UBS Optimus Foundation	Supports programs in child health, child protection and child education. Focuses on African countries including Liberia, Sierra Leone, Ivory Coast, Ghana and South Africa	Has supported 'School in a Box' in Ghana, Liberia and Sierra Leone and 'Happy Meals' in Uganda and Kenya	www.ubs.com/ global/en/wealth_ management/ optimus foundation
Village Capital	Operates business development programs for early-stage entrepreneurs in agriculture, education, energy, financial inclusion, and health and invests in the top two graduates from each program	Conducts training for entrepreneurs in Africa, has also invested in a number of businesses across East and West Africa	www.vilcap.com

Name of intiative	Sector focus and activities	Presence/activities in Africa	Website address
Wallace Global Fund	Supports transformative change and funds social movements that are working to challenge corporate power, defend and renew democracy, protect the environment, promote truth and creative freedom, and advance women's human rights and empowerment. Has supported initiatives in strengthening democracy and stopping female genital mutilation in Africa		www.wgf.org
William and Flora Hewlett Foundation	Makes grants to support research and initiatives in the following areas: education, environment, global development and population, performing arts and philanthropy	Has actively supported research institutions and projects in education and global development and population in Africa since 2001. Has made 18 grants in 2015, all in the global development and population category	www.hewlett.org

Prizes and awards

Name of award	Region	Summary of award	Amount	Website address
Africa Awards for Entrepreneurship (Outstanding Social Entrepreneur)	Africa	Dubbed the 'Oscars of Entrepreneurship in Africa', this prestigious award program identifies 13 of the leading entrepreneurs in Africa each year.	Varies (Over the last 7 years, AAE has attracted over 7,000 applications and awarded over $1.8m in prizes to 35 entrepreneurs)	www.africanleader shipnetwork.com/ aae/
Anzisha Prize	Africa	Awards young entrepreneurs under 25 years who have developed and implemented innovative solutions to social challenges or started successful businesses within their communities	$25,000 each for 3 grand prize winners	www.anzishaprize. org

Name of award	Region	Summary of award	Amount	Website address
D-Prize	Global	D-Prize is a call to the world's boldest entrepreneurs. Provides seed capital for launching social enterprises in Africa, India, or another other developing region. Awarded to 5-15 social entrepreneurs and helps them find future funding if their pilot is successful	$20,000	www.d-prize.org
Hivos Social Innovation Award	Global	Hivos uses social innovation as a framework to strive towards open and green societies	£125,000	www.hivossocial innovationaward. org
Hult Prize	Global	Start-up accelerator that aims to create and launch the most compelling social start-up enterprises that tackle grave issues faced by billions of people	$1 million	www.hultprize.org
Innovation Prize for Africa	Africa	Honours and encourages innovative achievements that contribute towards developing new products, increasing efficiency or saving cost in Africa	$150,000	www.innovation prizeforafrica.org/ about-ipa
Nestle Prize in Creating Shared Value	Global (focus on low-income countries)	Rewards initiatives addressing challenges in nutrition, water and rural development. Awarded biennially	CHF 500,000 (approx. $530,000)	www.nestle.com/ csv/what-is-csv/ nestleprize

Name of award	Region	Summary of award	Amount	Website address
ONE Africa Award	Africa	Recognizes Africa-driven, Africa led advocacy efforts that have demonstrated success at community, national or regional level towards achieving the Millennium Development Goals	$100,000	www.one.org/africa/the-one-africa-award
Orange African Social Venture Prize	Global	Aims to promote social innovation supporting development through communication and information technologies	€10,000–25,000	en.starafrica.com/entrepreneurship/orange-african-social-venture-prize-2014
SAB Foundation Social Innovation Awards	South Africa	Awarded for sustainable social innovation that addresses challenges faced by women, the youth, persons with disabilities and persons in rural areas. Emphasis is placed on innovations that are scalable and able to be commercialised	1st – R1.2 million 2nd – R600,000 3rd – R400,000 Seed grants between R100,000 and R150,000 for other deserving finalists	www.sab.co.za/sablimited/content/sab foundation-home
Sankalp Africa Awards	Africa	Recognizes and supports leading social enterprises on the African continent	Connects enterprises to funding opportunities of up to $1 million	www.sankalp forum.com/awards/sankalp-africa-awards-2015
Saville Foundation Pan-African Awards for Entrepreneurship in Education	Africa	Rewards organizations that contribute to Africa's long term growth and development through an entrepreneurial approach to education and training. Open to organizations based in Africa and working in education	$10,000	www.teachaman tofish.org.uk/pan-african-awards

Name of award	Region	Summary of award	Amount	Website address
SEED Awards for Entrepreneurship in Sustainable Development	Global	Annual awards scheme designed to find the most promising, innovative and locally led start-up social and environmental enterprises in countries with developing and emerging economies	Varies	www.seedinit.org/awards/about
Sukuma Afrika Young Entrepreneurs Competition	Africa	Recognizes entrepreneurs with enterprises that are contributing to the eradication of poverty and the attainment of the MDGs. Provides one-on-one networking opportunities for winners and alumni with potential funders that specialize in funding social entrepreneurs in Africa	N/A	www.sukuma afrika.org
Sustainia Award	Global	Sustainia Award is an annual international award given to a solution, technology or project with a significant potential to help build a more sustainable future	N/A	www.sustainia.me/sustainia-action-forum/
The Future Awards	Africa	Celebrates young people between the ages of 18 and 31, who have made an outstanding achievement in the year under consideration	Unknown	thefutureafrica.com/awards/about-us/
The Impumelelo Innovations Award Program	South Africa	'Shining a light on South African solutions to South African problems'	Varies	impumelelo.org.za/awards-programme/the-impumelelo-innovations-awards-programme

Name of award	Region	Summary of award	Amount	Website address
Transform Kenya Awards	Kenya	Transform Kenya Awards is a joint initiative of The Standard Group and Deloitte. Aims at recognizing and celebrating persons, organizations or institutions that are doing something remarkable to contribute to the positive transformation of the lives of the community at either grass roots or national level	Unknown	transformkenya awards.com/
Unilever Sustainable Living Young Entrepreneurs Awards/HRH The Prince of Wales Young Sustainability Entrepreneur Prize	Global	Focused on encouraging young people to come up with practical and innovative solutions to some of the world's biggest sustainability challenges	7 awardees get a total of €200,000	www.change makers.com/ sustliving2014
Zayed Future Energy Prize	Global	Recognizes individuals and organizations that have made significant contributions in the fields of renewable energy and sustainability. Also recognizes high schools	$4 million	www.zayedfuture energyprize.com

Leadership and networks

Name of initiative	Activities and sector focus	Presence and activities in Africa to date	Website address
Africa Leadership Institute	Mentorship, networking	Africa-wide, but based in South Africa, selects 20 fellows from across the continent each year	www.alinstitute.org
Bertha Centre for Social Innovation & Entrepreneurship	Environmental impact investment and scholarships for young social entrepreneurs to attend the University of Cape Town Graduate School of Business	Africa-wide, most current fellows are South African	www.gsb.uct.ac.za/ berthacentre
East African Social Entrepreneurship Network	Advocacy, business development and incubation	Focused on East Africa	easenetwork.net
Nexus Global Youth Summit	Brings together 2000+ young investors, social entrepreneurs and their allies for dialogue, education and collaborative problem solving	Organized summits in South Africa in 2013 and 2014 to increase young African philanthropy	www.nexusyouth summit.org
Sauder Social Entrepreneurship	Business education	Every summer, students from UBC and Strathmore University attempt to empower the underprivileged youths living in the most deprived parts of Nairobi with the skills to develop business plans	www.sauder.ubc.ca/ Global_Reach/ Sauder_Social_ Entrepreneurship_- _Kenya
The Synergos Institute	Technical assistance and capacity-building workshops, global network, mentorships	Economic development and poverty alleviation in North Africa	www.synergos.org

Fellowships

Name of initiative	Description	Eligibility criteria	Website address
Acumen Fund Global Fellows Program	12-month full-time fellowship for individuals dedicated to serving the poor and who have the business and operational expertise, and moral imagination needed to effect long-term social change	• Strong business experience: finance, operations, sales, marketing, and/or consulting • Demonstrated passion and commitment to creating positive social change • Proven track record of leadership and management responsibilities • Experience living and working in emerging markets • Grit, courage and perseverance • A minimum of 4 years work experience	www.acumen.org
Acumen East Africa Fellows Program	One-year leadership development program designed to build the next generation of social leaders, selects 20 fellows every year	• Innovators who either started an organization or enterprise, or who are driving change within an existing organization or company • East Africans who demonstrate a commitment and concrete connection to the region • Leaders with strong personal integrity, unrelenting perseverance and moral imagination • Committed individuals ready to undergo an intensive year-long personal transformation and leadership journey	www.acumen.org

Name of initiative	Description	Eligibility criteria	Website address
Allan Gray Orbis Foundation	Aims to develop students into Southern Africa's future high impact responsible entrepreneurs. Focused on South Africa, Namibia, Botswana and Swaziland	In selecting fellows, the Foundation assesses applicants against the following criteria: • achievement excellence • intellectual imagination • courageous commitment • spirit of significance and; • personal initiative	www.allangrayorbis.org
Ashoka	Designed for leading social entrepreneurs who have innovative solutions to social problems and the potential to change patterns across society	Ashoka fellows must have strong ethical backgrounds and their ideas must be: • new • creative • entrepreneurial • socially impactful	www.ashoka.org
Aspen Africa Leadership Initiative (ALI)	A collaborative effort of 7 partner organizations in Africa and the United States, focused on fostering values-based, action-oriented leadership in Africa	ALI fellows are highly successful, entrepreneurial individuals from business, government and civil society	www.aspen institute.org/ leadership-programs/africa-leadership-initiative
Echoing Green Global Fellowship	Program for emerging social entrepreneurs, awarded annually	Applicants must be: • over 18 years old • fluent in english • able to commit a full 35 hour work week to their organization. Their organizations must be: • the original idea of the applicant(s) • in its start-up phase, usually within the first two years of operation • independent and autonomous	www.echoing green.org

Name of initiative	Description	Eligibility criteria	Website address
Ibrahim Leadership Fellowship	A selective program designed to mentor future African leaders. Fellows receive mentoring from the current leaders of key multilateral institutions.	• national of an African country • 7–10 years of relevant work experience • master's degree • under the age of 40, or 45 for women with children	www.moibrahim foundation.org
Rainer Arnhold Fellowship (Mulago Foundation)	The program helps social entrepreneurs design their programs for maximum impact and scale	The program seeks fellows that have an entrepreneurial personality and proven track record, lead an existing organization, have an interest in scalable design, possess a degree of decision-making authority, a thorough understanding of their design process and tools and have an openness to new ideas and the willingness to change course	www.mulago foundation.org
Social Entrepreneurs Transforming Africa	Year-long fellowship being implemented by Makerere University Business School in collaboration with the International Youth Foundation (IYF), the United States Agency for International Development (USAID), and The MasterCard Foundation.	Open to 25 young leaders (ages 18 to 29) who have founded or co-founded a venture that addresses a social challenge in their communities	www.setafrica.org

Name of initiative	Description	Eligibility criteria	Website address
Unreasonable Network Fellowship	Provides entrepreneurs with what they need to scale solutions to the world's biggest problems at diverse, in person programs (ranging from 5 days to 5 weeks). Has an East African Institute in Uganda which unites 10–20 entrepreneurs under one roof for 4–5 weeks to receive training and mentorship	• operates in Uganda, Kenya or Tanzania (for the 5-week program, open to all countries for the 5-day program) • are for-profit or nonprofit • have achieved significant traction in their market • have released their product/service, gained feedback from their target population, and then developed their product to better meet the demand • have a strong business model	unreasonable eastafrica.org

Social entrepreneurship training and incubation programs

Name of program	Location	Offering	Timelines and duration	Cost	Website address
African Leadership Academy (Catalyst term)	South Africa	A study abroad experience for international students in Johannesburg that aims to develop catalysts of positive social change	Catalyst term 1: (16 weeks) Catalyst term 2: (21 weeks) Catalyst year: (37 weeks)	Catalyst term 1: $20,000 Catalyst term 2: $23,000 Catalyst year: $40,000	catalyst. african leadership academy. org

Name of program	Location	Offering	Timelines and duration	Cost	Website address
Amani Institute	Kenya	**Post-Graduate Certificate in Social Innovation Management:** a personalized, field-based program that brings together a diverse group of like-minded individuals all passionate about building the professional and personal skills to lead change and create positive impact	Duration: 4 months	$5,950 for participants from Nairobi	www.amani institute.org
Bertha Centre for Social Innovation & Entrepre-neurship	South Africa	First academic centre in Africa dedicated to advancing social innovation and entrepreneurship. Offers scholarship to social innovators to study at the Bertha Centre at the Graduate School of Business at the University of Cape Town	Scholarship applications should be submitted the year before entry	N/A	www.gsb.uct. ac.za/s.asp? p=389
Co-Creation Hub (CcHUB)	Nigeria	Tech-In-Series, developers Parapo, Nokia-CcHUB Growth Academy and other periodic training programs for social entrepreneurs utilizing technology to solve social issues	N/A	Usually free	www.cchubnig eria.com

Name of program	Location	Offering	Timelines and duration	Cost	Website address
East Africa Social Enterprise (EASE) Network	Kenya	• social entrepreneurship • social enterprise development • social enterprise business planning • finance for non-finance managers • microfinance and microenterprise • project cycle management	N/A	N/A	www.ease network.com
Fuqua School of Business, Duke University – Centre for the Advance-ment of Social Entre-preneurship		Prepares leaders and organizations with the business skills needed to achieve lasting social change through elective courses on the MBA program. Courses include: Social entrepreneurship, impact investing etc.	N/A	N/A	centers.fuqua. duke.edu/case/
Google for Entre-preneurs	Varies	Brings together start-up communities and creates spaces for entrepreneurs to learn and work. Also provides financial support and resources to start-up communities that equip and nurture entrepreneurs	N/A	N/A	www.googlefor entrepreneurs. com

Name of program	Location	Offering	Timelines and duration	Cost	Website address
Haas School of Business, University of California, Berkeley	USA	**Social sector solutions (S3):** Provides MBA students with top-quality consulting projects that address pressing social issues for clients in the nonprofit, public and social enterprise sectors	N/A	N/A	socialsector. haas.berkeley. edu/
		Philanthropy University: Provides free online education to social change-makers working to make the world a better place. Participants earn a certificate of completion in social impact leadership	Always available online	Free	novoed.com/ philanthropy-initiative
Harvard Business School (Social Enterprise)	USA	• nonprofit strategy and governance • business for social impact • K-12 education • impact investing	N/A	N/A	www.hbs. edu/social enterprise/
Impact Hub	Accra Bamako Harare Johannesburg Khartoum Kigali	Africa seed program	Duration: 6 months	Unknown	africa.impact hub.net

Name of program	Location	Offering	Timelines and duration	Cost	Website address
Kellogg School of Management, Northwestern University	USA	**SEEK: Social Enterprise at Kellogg:** Offers a range of courses designed to help MBA students build the skillsets required to become socially responsible leaders. Also offers seed funding through the Kellogg Social Entrepreneurship Award which provides a $70,00 award and ongoing support from the Levy Entrepreneurship Lab	N/A	N/A	www.kellogg. northwestern. edu/ departments/ seek.aspx
LEAP Africa's Social Innovators Program	Nigeria	Offers a competitive one-year fellowship to 20 young social innovators operating in Nigeria. Provides training, coaching and publicity	One year	Free	www.leap africa.org
Microsoft 4Afrika School of Government	N/A	Interactive workshops designed for senior government leaders responsible for developing and implementing IT policy	N/A	N/A	www.micro soft.com/ africa/4afrika/ academy/ school-of- government. aspx

Name of program	Location	Offering	Timelines and duration	Cost	Website address
Microsoft Virtual Academy 4Afrika	Online	Courses on technology and business. Provides a unique way for students to learn and interact online with experts from across the African continent	Varies	Free	www.microsoft .com/africa/ 4afrika/acade my/virtual-academy.aspx
Philanthropy University	Online	Courses offered: • Leadership: ten rules for impact and meaning • How to scale social impact • Fundraising: how to connect with donors • Financial modelling for the social sector • Global social entrepreneurship • Organizational capacity: assessment to action • Essentials of nonprofit strategy	Varies	Free	novoed.com/ philanthropy-initiative
Ross School of Business, University of Michigan	USA	Focused on empowering leaders with practical skills and insight to tackle complex social challenges	N/A	N/A	socialimpact. umich.edu/

Name of program	Location	Offering	Timelines and duration	Cost	Website address
Said Business School – Skoll Centre for Social Entrepreneurship	Oxford, UK	Seeks to foster innovative social transformation through education, research and collaboration. Also offers the Skoll Scholarship for incoming MBA students who are currently pursuing entrepreneurial solutions for urgent social and environmental challenges	N/A	N/A	www.sbs.ox. ac.uk/faculty-research/skoll
Spark Change-makers Program	Kenya, South Africa and Tanzania (planned)	Intensive 5 day workshop in Johannesburg/ Nairobi designed to help early-stage South African/ Kenyan social entrepreneurs. Expected to help them focus and accelerate their venture	Consult website	Free	www.spark international. org
SHE by Spark Change-makers	Kenya South Africa	A unique accelerator program designed to find and support female entrepreneurs that are improving the lives of women and girls in South Africa and Kenya	Consult website		

Name of program	Location	Offering	Timelines and duration	Cost	Website address
Stanford Graduate School of Business, Centre for Social Innovation	USA	Courses offered: • Certificate in public management and social innovation • Executive program in social entrepreneurship • Program on social entrepreneurship	Varies	Varies	www.gsb.stanford.edu/faculty-research/centers-initiatives/csi www.gsb.stanford.edu/programs/executive-program-social-entrepreneurship
Unreasonable Institute East Africa	Uganda Kenya Tanzania	Five-week accelerator program based in Uganda for early-stage entrepreneurs tackling the world's most pressing social and environmental challenges	Varies	$13,000 ($3,000 upfront and the balance phased over an agreed period of time)	www.unreasonableeastafrica.org/
Unreasonable Labs	Ghana Morocco	Five-day accelerators for early-stage entrepreneurs tackling the world's most pressing social and environmental challenges. Focuses on certain sub-themes e.g. business model validation, investment preparedness etc.	Varies	$100–500 (Depends on the country)	www.unreasonablelabs.org/home/ghana/

Name of program	Location	Offering	Timelines and duration	Cost	Website address
Yale School of Management	USA	The Program on social enterprise (PSE) helps social entrepreneurs harness business skills to achieve social objectives. Provides elective courses on social enterprise that are incorporated into the school's MBA curriculum	N/A	N/A	som.yale.edu/ faculty- research/our- centers/ program- social- enterprise/ programs

Challenge funds

Name of fund	Key funders	Description	Website address
Africa Enterprise Challenge Fund (AECF)	UK Department of International Development (DFID)	Has held 18 funding competitions, and, as of May 2015, allocated approximately $244 million to 208 private sector companies focused on agriculture. Funding is expected to be matched by the wining companies. Focus is on practical projects that are both commercially viable and have a broad developmental impact on the rural poor	www.aecfafrica.org
All Children Reading	USAID, Australian Aid	An ongoing series of competitions that leverages science and technology to create and apply scalable solutions to improve literacy skills of early grade learners in developing countries. First round of winners included organizations in South Sudan, South Africa, Malawi, and other African countries	www.allchildren reading.org
Fighting Ebola	USAID	Established to help healthcare workers on the front lines provide better care and stop the spread of Ebola through a range of solutions that range from solutions that should enable longer work periods; require less personal protective equipment (PPE) and fewer transitions; provide cleaner work environments; and generate less infectious waste and/or offer enhanced protection for disposal of waste	www.usaid.gov/ grandchallenges/ ebola

Name of fund	Key funders	Description	Website address
Grand Challenges	Bill & Melinda Gates Foundation	Includes a family of initiatives fostering innovation to solve key global health and development problems. Over 200 grants have been awarded across Africa (2015)	www.grandchallenges. org
Innovations Against Poverty	Swedish International Development Cooperation Agency (SIDA)	Propels the private sector to develop products, services and business models that can contribute to poverty reduction and combat climate change	www.sida.se/English/ partners/resources-for-all-partners/ Challenge-Funds/ Innovations-Against-Poverty/
Making All Voices Count	USAID, SIDA, DfID and Omidyar Network	Supports people and governments to use innovation, web and mobile technologies to improve government performance and accountability. Works in 12 countries across Africa and Asia	www.makingallvoices count.org
Powering Agriculture	USAID, the Swedish International Development Cooperation Agency (SIDA), the German Federal Ministry for Economic Cooperation and Development (BMZ), Duke Energy, and the Overseas Private Investment Corporation (OPIC)	Encourages innovators to find new ways to bring clean energy to farmers through sustainable and scalable solutions that will create more and better quality food for farmers, their families and their communities. 61% of supported projects are implemented in Africa	www.PoweringAg.org

Name of fund	Key funders	Description	Website address
Saving Lives at Birth	USAID, the government of Norway, the Bill & Melinda Gates Foundation, Grand Challenges Canada, The World Bank, and the UK Department for International Development (DFID)	Established to support groundbreaking prevention and treatment approaches for pregnant women and newborns in poor, low resource communities around the 48 hours of delivery. Has supported innovators in Kenya and Nigeria.	www.savinglivesat birth.net
Securing Water for Food	USAID, Swedish International Development Cooperation Agency (SIDA)	Supports scientific and technological innovations to more effectively use and manage the water required to produce food in developing and emerging countries. Has supported projects in Kenya, South Sudan, Ethiopa, Uganda, and other African countries	www.securingwaterfor food.org
TradeMark East Africa Challenge Fund	TradeMark East Africa (TMEA)	Focused on promoting cross-border trade in East Africa ultimately to boost trade and stimulate economic growth in the region	www.trac-fund.com

References

Altangerel, Tuya and Chanmi Kim. 2013. *Guidance Note: Scaling Up Development Programmes*. New York: United Nations Development Programme.

A.T. Kearney. 2014. *Investment and Finance Study for Off-Grid Lighting*. Netherlands: GOGLA.

Academy for Educational Development. 2004. *Going to SCALE: System-wide Collaborative Action for Livelihoods and the Environment*. Accessed on June 5th 2015. Available at: www.ircwash.org/sites/default/files/AED-2004-Going.pdf

AlliedCrowds. 2015. *Developing World Crowfunding: Sustainability through Crowdfunding*. Accessed on August 5th 2015. Available at: http://alliedcrowds.com/assets/July-2015.pdf

Berelowitz, Dan, Pranav Chopra, Greg Coussa, Martha Paren, Matt Towner, Hettle Wetherill, and Jon Huggett. 2015. *Social Replication Toolkit*. International Centre for Social Franchising.

Berelowitz, Dan, Mark Richardson and Matt Towner. 2013. *Realising the Potential of Social Replication*. The International Centre for Social Franchising.

Bhattacharyya, Onil, Will Mitchell, Anita McGahan, Kate Mossman, Leigh Hayden, Jason Sukhram, David Leung, *et al.* 2015. *Rapid Route to Scale: Scaling up Primary Care to Improve Health in Low and Middle Income Countries*. International Centre for Social Franchising.

Bloom, Paul N. and Aaron K. Chatterji. 2008. *Scaling Social Entrepreneurial Impact*. Accessed on April 20th 2016. Available at: https://faculty.fuqua.duke.edu/~ronnie/bio/BloomChatterji_090108.pdf

Bridge IMPACT+ and African Private Equity and Venture Capital Association (AVCA). 2014. *Investing for impact: A strategy of choice for African Policymakers*. London: Bridge Ventures LLP.

The Bridgespan Group. 2013. *From Start-up to Scale: Conversations from the Harvard Business Review Bridgespan Insight Center on Scaling Social Impact*. Accessed on April 20th 2016. Available at: www.bridgespan.org/getmedia/2e3147b3-939e-45b7-b7b2-dd7c959e1d9f/From-Start-up-to-Scale.pdf.aspx

Brown, Ashley C., Jon Stern and Bernard Tenenbaum. 2006. *Handbook for Evaluating Infrastructure Regulatory Systems*. Washington DC: The World Bank.

Call, Carolyn Sherwood. 2012. 'Financial Innovations in Social Enterprise'. *Evolving Models: Innovations in Social Enterprise*. Center for Socially Responsible Business, Lorry I. Lokey Graduate School of Business, Mills College.

Cambridge associates (CA) and Global Impact Investing Network (GIIN). 2015. *Introducing the Impact Investing Benchmark*. Cambridge, MA: Cambridge Associates LLC.

The Case Foundation. 2012. *To Be Fearless*. Accessed on 20th April 2016. Available at: http://casefoundation.org/wp-content/uploads/2014/11/ToBeFearless.pdf

Castellano, Antonio, Adam Kendall, Mikhail Nikomarov and Tarryn Swemmer. 2015. *Brighter Africa: The Growth Potential of the Sub-Saharan Electricity Sector*. McKinsey & Company.

Chandy, Laurence, Akio Hosono, Homi Kharas and Johannes Linn. 2013. *Getting to Scale: How to Bring Development Solutions to Millions of Poor People*. Washington DC: Brookings Institution Press.

Chase, Jenny. 2014. *Offgrid Solar: Show Me the Money*. Bloomberg Finance L.P.

Civicus. 2015. *State of Civil Society Report*. Civicus: World Alliance for Citizen Participation.

Clayton, Tonika Cheek. 2008. *Case Study No. 6: Principles for Effective Education Grant-making*. Portland, OR: Grantmakers for Education.

Cooley, Larry, and Richard Kohl. 2012. *Scaling Up—From Vision to Large Scale Change: A Management Framework for Practitioners*. Washington DC: Management Systems International.

Cooley, Larry and Johannes F. Linn. 2014. *Taking Innovations to Scale: Methods, Application and Lessons*. Washington DC: Results for Development Institute.

Dalberg Global Development Advisors. 2014. *Transforming Secondary Education in Nigeria*. Accessed on April 20th 2016. Available at: www.dalberg.com/wp-content/uploads/2015/07/Transforming-Secondary-School-Education-in-Nigeria.pdf

Development Impact Bond Working Group. 2013. *Investing in Social Outcomes Development Impact Bonds*. Center for Global Development & Social Finance UK.

Doss, Henry and Alistair Brett. 2015. *The Rainforest Scorecard: A Practical Framework for Growing Innovation Potential*. Los Altos, CA: Regenwald.

E.T. Jackson and Associates Ltd. 2012. *Accelerating Impact: Achievements, Challenges and What's Next in Building the Impact Investing Industry*. The Rockefeller Foundation.

ExpandNet and World Health Organization. 2012. *Worksheets for Developing a Scaling strategy*. Accessed on August 10th 2015. Available at: www.expandnet.net/PDFs/ExpandNet-WHO%20Worksheets%20-%20July%202012.pdf

FLHE Unit, Federal Ministry of Education. 2012. *2009–2011 National Family Life HIV/AIDS Education (NFLHE) Curriculum Implementation Result*.

Gabriel, Madeleine. 2014. *Making it Big: Social Strategies for Scaling Social Innovations*. NESTA.

Global Impact. 2013. *Assessment of US Giving to International Causes*. Accessed on May 5th 2016. Available at: http://charity.org/sites/default/files/userfiles/pdfs/Assessment%20of%20US%20Giving%20to%20International%20Causes%20FINAL.pdf

Global Impact Investing Network. 2015. *The Landscape for Impact Investing in Africa*. Accessed on April 20th 2016. Available at: https://thegiin.org/knowledge/publication/westafricareport

Googins, Bradley K. 2014. *E4Impact Africa: Pilot Project Evaluation*. ALTIS.

Grossman, Allen. 2013. *Developing a Social Enterprise Business Plan*. Massachusetts: President & Fellows of Harvard College.

Guay, Justin, Carl Pope, Jigar Shah and Stewart Craine. 2014. *Expanding Energy Access Beyond the Grid: Five Principles for Designing Off-Grid and Mini-Grid Policy*. Sierra Club.

Hausmann, Ricardo, César A. Hidalgo, Sebastián Bustos, Michele Coscia, Sarah Chung, Juan Jimenez, Alexander Simoes and Muhammed A. Yıldırım. 2011. *The Atlas of Economic Complexity: Mapping Paths to Prosperity*. New Hampshire: Puritan Press.

Huaynoca, Silvia, Venkatraman Chandra-Mouli, Nuhu Yaqub Jr., and Donna Marie Denno. 2014. 'Scaling up Comprehensive Sexuality Education in Nigeria: From National Policy to Nationwide Application'. *Sex Education*, 14(2): 191–209.

The Impact Programme. 2015. *Survey of the Impact Investment Market 2014: Challenges and Opportunities in Sub-Saharan Africa and South Asia.* Accessed on April 20th 2016. Available at: www.theimpactprogramme.org.uk/resources/

International Finance Corporation. 2012. *From Gap to Opportunity: Business Models for Scaling Up Energy Access.* International Finance Corporation.

International Food Policy Research Institute. 2012. *Scaling Up in Agriculture, Rural Development, and Nutrition.* Policy Briefs, International Food Policy Research Institute.

Jideofor, Nonso. 2014. *Enabling Citizen-Driven Improvements of Public Services in Nigeria.* REBOOT.

Juma, Calestous. 2011. *The New Harvest: Agricultural Innovation in Africa.* New York: Oxford University Press, Inc.

Kalafatas, John. n.d. *Approaches to Scaling Social Impact.* Duke University: Center for the Advancement of Social Entrepreneurship. Accessed on June 6th 2015. Available at: www.socialimpactexchange.org/files/publications/approaches_toscaling_social_impact.pdf

Keohane, Levenson Georgia. 2013. *Social Entrepreneurship for the 21st Century: Innovation Across the Nonprofit, Private and Public Sectors.* McGraw Hill.

Khalid Malik *et al.* 2014. Sustaining Human Progress: Reducing Vulnerabilities and Building Resilience. *Human Development Report 2014.* New York: United Nations Development Programme.

Koh, Harvey, Nidhi Hegde and Ashish Karamchandani. 2014. *Beyond the Pioneer: Getting Inclusive Industries to Scale.* Deloitte Touche Tohmatsu India Private Limited.

Legatum Institute. 2014. *The 2014 Africa Prosperity Report.* Accessed on April 20th 2016. Available at: www.li.com/activities/publications/2014-africa-prosperity-report

Leviner, Noga, Leslie R. Crutchfield and Diana Wells. 2007. *Understanding the Impact of Social Entrepreneurs Ashoka's Answer to the Challenge of Measuring Effectiveness.* Accessed 20th April 2016. Available at: www.ashoka.org/sites/ashoka/files/UnderstandingtheImpactChapterPDF.pdf

Lewis, Suzanne Grant, Jonathan Friedman and John Schoneboom. 2010. *Accomplishments of the Partnership for Higher Education in Africa, 2000–2010.* New York: New York University.

Lighting Africa. 2011. *The Off-Grid Lighting Market in Sub-Saharan Africa: Market Research Synthesis Report.* International Financial Corporation and the World Bank.

Major, Dara. 2011. *What Do We Mean by Scale?* Grantmakers for Effective Organization.

Meader, David K. 2013. 'Innovative Funding Opportunities for Social Enterprises: The Insiders Guide to Raising Money'. *CSRB Insights,* December 15, (2)2.

Milligan, Katherine. *et al.* 2013. *Breaking the Binary: Policy Guide to Scaling Social Innovation.* Geneva: Schwab Foundation for Social Entrepreneurship.

Mirza, Hafiz, William Speller, Grahame Dixie, and Zoë Goodman. 2014. *The Practice of Responsible Investment Principles in Larger Scale Agricultural Investments: Implications for Corporate Performance and Impact on Local Communities.* World Bank Report N86175-GLB. Agriculture and Environmental Services Discussion Paper 08. Washington: The World Bank

Mudaliar, Abhilash and Lauren Barra. 2015. *ImpactBase Snapshot: An Analysis of 300+ Impact Investing Funds.* New York: Global Impact Investing Network.

Mulgan, Geoff, Rushanara Ali, Richard Halkett and Ben Sanders. 2007. *In and Out of Sync: The Challenge of Growing Social Innovations.* NESTA.

Ohiri, Kelechi. 2015. 'Developing and Scaling Healthcare Innovations in Africa: Experiences from Nigeria'. Presentation made at the Harvard Kennedy School, as part of Ndidi Nwuneli's MRCBG Fellowship.

One Acre Fund. 2014. *Scale Innovations*. Accessed on May 10th 2015. Available at: www.oneacrefund.org/uploads/all-files/White_Paper_-_Social_Enterprise_-_Scale _Innovations_FINAL.pdf

Roberts, Peter W., Sean Peters and Saurabh Lall. 2014. *The Impact of Entrepreneurship Database Program: 2014 Mid-Year Data Summary*. Social Enterprise Goizueta.

Roob, Nancy and Jeffrey L. Bradach. 2009. *Scaling What Works: Implications for Philan-thropists, Policymakers, and Nonprofit Leaders*. The Bridgespan Group.

Rose, Amy, Andrew Campanell, Reja Amatya and Robert Stoner. 2015. *Solar Power Applications in the Developing World*. MIT Energy Initiative.

Saltuk, Yasemin. 2015. *Eyes on the Horizon: The Impact Investor Survey*. JP Morgan Chase & Co.

Sankalp Forum. 2014. *Sankalp Africa Summit: Post Event Report*. Intellecap.

Simmons, Ruth, Laura Ghiron and Peter Fajans. 2010. *Nine Steps for Developing a Scaling-up Strategy*. Geneva: World Health Organization Press.

So, Ivy and Alina Staskevicius. 2015. *Measuring the 'Impact' in Impact Investing*. Harvard Business School.

Sodzi-Tettey, S., N.A.Y Twum-Danso, L.N. Mobisson-Etuk, L.H. Macy, J. Roessner and P.M. Barker. 2015. *Lessons Learned from Ghana's Project Fives Alive! A Practical Guide for Designing and Executing Large-Scale Improvement Initiatives*. Cambridge, MA.: Institute for Healthcare Improvement.

Strongminds and Katia Peterson. 2014. *End of Phase One Impact Evaluation for the Treating Depression at Scale in Africa Program in Uganda*. Accessed 20th April 2015. Available at: http://strongminds.org/wp-content/uploads/2014/11/StrongMinds-Impact-Evaluation-Report-November-2014.pdf

Syngenta Foundation for Sustainable Agriculture. 2014. *Growing Smartly: Scaling Seed Systems and the Adoption of Agricultural Technologies Among Smallholder Farmers*. Switzerland: Syngenta Foundation Press.

Tam, Vikki *et al.* 2014. *Growing Prosperity: Developing Repeatable Models to Scale the Adoption of Agricultural Innovations*. Acumen and Brain & Company Inc.

Tyler, Geoff and Grahame Dixie. 2013. *Investing in Agribusiness: A Retrospective View of a Development Bank's Investments in Agribusiness in Africa and Southeast Asia and the Pacific*. Washington DC: The World Bank.

UK Social Investment Task Force. 2000. *Enterprising Communities: Wealth Beyond Welfare*. London. Accessed 20th April 2015. Available at: www.ronaldcohen.org/sites/default/ files/3/SITF_Oct_2000.pdf

Volans Ventures Ltd. 2015. *The Stretch Agenda: Breakthrough in the Boardroom*. London: Volans Ventures Ltd.

The World Bank. 2014. *Agribusiness Indicators: Synthesis Report*. Agriculture Global Practice Discussion Paper 01. Accessed 20th April 2016. Available at: http://goo.gl/PlIojd

The World Bank. 2014. *Doing Business 2015: Going Beyond Efficiency*. 12th Edition. A World Bank Group Flagship report. Accessed 20th April 2016. Available at: www.doingbusiness.org/~/media/GIAWB/Doing%20Business/Documents/Annual-Reports/English/DB15-Full-Report.pdf

World Health Organisation. 2008. *Scaling Up Health Services: Challenges and Choices*. Accessed 20 April 2016. Technical Brief No 3. Available at: www.who.int/health-systems/topics/delivery/technical_brief_scale-up_june12.pdf

Yunus, Muhammad, Bertrand Moingeon and Laurence Lehmann-Ortega. 2010. 'Building Social Business Models: Lessons from the Grameen Experience'. *Long Range Planning*, 308–325.

Index

Note: Page references in bold font indicate figures and tables.